cover: "Home Sweet Home"
Winslow Homer c.1863
oil on canvas, National Gallery

Leu Bradley Jr
1st. Serjt. Co. B. 1st. Mass. H. Art.
2nd Brig. 3d Div. 2d Corps.
Army of the Potomac
1865.

LEVERETT BRADLEY:
A SOLDIER-BOY'S LETTERS,
1862-1865

edited and introduction by
Susan Hinckley Bradley

forward by
Dan Gagnon
author of *Methuen: An Eclectic History*

SICPRESS 2012
METHUEN, MASS.

Leverett Bradley's letters were orginally published in 1905 as *"Leverett Bradley; a soldier-boy's letters, 1862-1865"* as part of a combined volume with a post-humous sermon *"The Priesthood: a man's work in the ministry"* by Phillips Brooks.

Cover illustration is "Home Sweet Home" by Winslow Homer c.1863 oil on canvas, from the National Gallery, Washington, D.C.

series edited by J. Godsey
for copies sales@SicPress.com
Methuen, MA 2012

Table of Contents

Forward to the New Edition 7

Introduction 9

A Soldier-Boy's Letters 1862-1865 17

Forward to the New Edition

Leverett Bradley Jr. served in Company B nearly 4 years and was witness to some of the most intense fighting of the Civil War. He was 15 years old when he joined his father's military unit as part of Company B, 1st Massachusetts Heavy Artillery. During this time he wrote home constantly. Early in the war he wrote about the boredom of camp life and constantly reassured his mother and sister that he was safe. For a person so young his letters were wonderfully written and gave the impression that he wanted to share his experiences with those that he loved. Though he never admitted homesickness he often requested things from home that made his life in camp a bit more homelike. As the war progressed, Leverett's letters changed. He became a participant in the horrors of war and his letters reflected that. They conveyed mostly a listing of events with little of the emotional sharing of earlier in the war. It was left to others to tell the stories of what he experienced .

Leverett, Jr. was eventually joined by his eleven year old brother Jerry, a drummer, later bugler. They were following a military tradition that dated back to before the American Revolution. Ancestors had fought at the Battle of Bunker Hill and in the Continental army. It would come as no surprise that his father continued this tradition by serving at one time as captain of the famed 6th Massachusetts Militia. Leverett, Jr. survived the war. He had been slightly wounded on more than one occasion and mustered out as a first lieutenant. History has shown that the horrors of war can leave scars on adolescent minds. Some struggled in life, suffering what today is diagnosed as Post Traumatic Stress Disorder. Others found mutual support in joining veterans' organization. Leverett Jr., though, turned to the church. He eventually found his calling as a minister in the Episcopal Church and died in 1902. As a memorial to him, his widow, Susan Hinckley Bradley privately published these letters and some sermons written in his honor in 1905.

Dan Gagnon
Methuen, 2012

Introduction

Catherine Frye, was born in Methuen, Massachusetts, July on the ancestral farm, situated on the banks of the Merrimac. The house in which he was born was begun at the time of the Revolution, but not finished, as is shown by the effect of the weather on the frame of hewn oak timbers, which were exposed during the years that the men were absent fighting for independence. In those days it must have been an imposing building, for in Leverett's boyhood it was a landmark for miles around.

The family, on his father's side, living at Haverhill, Massachusetts, was conspicuous in the early struggle of the colony and took an active part in all the movements for its defence. His great-grandfather, Enoch Bradley, was an officer in the Revolutionary War; his grandfather, Brickett Bradley, was a captain of dragoons in the early part of the nineteenth century. The latter was born and lived in the old Bradley homestead, where he is remembered for his energy, good cheer, and hospitality, as being a good friend and wise adviser.

The first son of Brickett Bradley and Hannah Merrill was named Leverett, after a friend, Leverett Saltonstall of Haverhill. When he was twenty-one his father gave him the farm and house which he had bought from the Fryes, and when he married Catherine C. Frye he brought her to the house built by her own grandfather. Leverett Bradley was known for his tenacity and clear-cut expression of thought and purpose. He could plan; he loved the excitement of big enterprises but was impatient of details, and here was perhaps the secret of his never making more than a comfortable living. He was free from all suspiciousness, and he did not reap the benefits of the plans he set in motion. When he was occupied with mechanical work, however, his accuracy was proverbial. He reclaimed and "made" the most valuable parts of the farm. His was a restless, progressive temperament, which re-belled at delay, and, always an optimist, he carried projects to a conclusion that would have staggered more conservative minds. He was very pure-minded, had a fine erect figure, and cleanness of speech. His love of music was one of his keenest pleasures, and he had a sweet tenor voice. As captain in the old Sixth Massachusetts Militia, Mr. Bradley's clear head and executive ability were recognized by his townspeople. When the Pemberton Mill in Lawrence fell he was at once chosen to take command and organize the volunteers to rescue the victims. His measures were at first thought severe, but in the light of further developments were recognized as far-sighted and wise. He had a strong constitution, was a bundle of nerves as far as work was concerned, and knew nothing of rest; but when finally forced to yield to pain, he bore his sufferings with fortitude till death relieved him, when he was sixty-six years old.

On his mother's side Leverett, Jr., also had the traditions of patriotism, his great-great-grandfather, Col. James Frye,* having commanded a regiment at the battle of Bunker Hill. His grandfather, Jeremiah Frye, owned many acres of farm-land and sold large tracts, among them part of the site of the present city of Lawrence.

Leverett remembered best his grandmother, Mrs. Jeremiah Frye, who was noted far and wide for her sweet and alert brightness, which spoke from her eyes. All felt the refinement of speech, accuracy of pronunciation, gracious courtesy of man-

---

*Colonel James Frye was born January 24, 1711, in Andover, Massachusetts. He died January 8, 1776, from the eflFects of a woimd received during the battle of Bunker Hill. He lived in Andover, and was colonel of the Fourth Essex Regiment, of which he was in command at the battle of Bunker Hill.

ner, of this rare old gentlewoman. With these was blended a charming wisdom, which expressed itself in fascinating epigrams quoted long years afterwards. She was the mother of a large family, and a busy worker. The home stood in the crossroads opposite the old church in which gathered weekly the large congregations of Methuen. In the long noons of the hot summers and in the cold winters Mrs. Frye's big-hearted hospitality welcomed the fathers, the mothers, the young men and maidens, of the town. Her wisdom was not acquired from book-learning; she studied life at first hand and understood the human heart. Young men admired and respected her; her children adored her; while in her grandsons she inspired a beautiful, chivalrous devotion.

Catherine, Leverett's mother, was Mrs. Frye's second daughter, and was bonnie and strong. Her strength and sunny, cheerful patience enabled her to accomplish an amount of work which would stagger the young mother of to-day. She never lost her gentleness and refinement and beautiful hospitality through long years of hard work in circumstances which required close economy. She took the personal care of her five children, besides the management of the entire household, which at times numbered from ten to twelve "hired men" that Mr. Bradley had engaged in his extensive improvements on the farm. At one time she baked a barrel of flour a week. She invariably met all the trials of her life with placid cheerfulness and never seemed to worry about possible ills; but in looking forward there was always before her mental vision a picture of physical danger and of privation for those she loved. This she often expressed, though ready at the first word to smile over her own apprehensions. She was the sunniest of pessimists. In later years she was often congratulated on the fine characters of all her children, and told that it was unusual to have no bad boys out of four. She invariably replied that she had never had a moment's anxiety in that respect; that they none of them had ever given her the slightest cause to do so; and then, fearing she had not been modest enough, she would add with a light heart, "There's time yet."

Leverett revered his mother more and more as the years went by, and marveled at her courage and vigor. She lived to be eighty-four, and when leisure came in her latter years she would sit reading, or embroidering and knitting, turning out good work, as she always had.

But no picture of the home and of Mrs. Bradley is complete without Lizzie, her oldest child and precious right hand. She entered into and shared her mother's life in all its details. From the time she was three years old she was a caretaker of the boys. She had so large an influence in forming Leverett's character that I quote, from an intimate cousin in the family, the following description "I have never known a more symmetrically developed character, one who exemplified in hourly living the principles which governed Jesus Christ, or one that made you feel so absolutely that to her own consciousness she emphasized all the good in you and dropped the bad out of sight. Yet she never gave the impression that she condoned evil, never! She rarely offered advice, though her advice was often sought, and in any real moral difficulty she almost always advised the course it was hard to pursue; but she seemed to give the strength to follow the best way. Her sympathy, insight, and discretion were wonderful. You never knew whether it was head or heart that spoke. Her definite intention seemed to control her as well as her emotions. She once told me that she had trained herself not to see. 'I used to be able to tell everything in a room after entering it; and in meeting a person I knew every detail of the dress worn.' Her love of the beautiful in nature was a passion, her appreciation of tasteful appointments was deep and refined, yet she never appeared to mind that she must herself forego the fine things she enjoyed. She was truly generous; she would have loved to give, but I never heard her deplore her inability to make gifts; indeed, she taught us that we need not have money or gear in order to give and to serve. She never failed one in trouble; she nursed the sick, comforted the sorrowing, and strengthened the weak outside the home; but it was in the home that she shone. Here she and Aunt Katie worked together. 'Bradley Farm' was loved by the relatives and friends far and near. Those who knocked at the door were made welcome with perfect hospitality, however unseasonable and inconvenient the call, however busy with pressing care their hands might be. Being on the road from Haverhill to Lawrence, it was not an uncommon occurrence to have a party drive up just as the family were rising from the dinner-table, the supply of provisions practically exhausted; but the welcome was so hearty that the inopportune arrivals had not a question about the lunch of delicious bread and butter, omelet, etc., that was hastily prepared and served, Lizzie enlivening all with her fun and dry way of saying things.

"Lizzie's friends passed their happiest days at the farm; each was left to do just as she pleased, but was never left to feel neglected. The boys would rather go home than anywhere else for their good times. And Lizzie kept their development and training in the little courtesies of life in mind. When they were absent she would go into the pasture, catch the horse, harness it, and drive into the city to do her father's errands; but were one of her brothers there he must fold her shawl about her, assist her to mount into the wagon or carriage; 'For,' she said, 'if they always have to wait on mother and me they will not forget to do these things when they have wives.' She was tireless in her love and devotion to her own, and when she passed out from the dear old home her going left a sorrow which graved indelible lines in the faces of those whom she left to prize her sweet, noble example and love her precious memory."

The oldest son was George, who took care of the home during the war and still lives on part of the old farm. Leverett was the second son, and was two years younger than George and two years older than his brother Jerry Payson, who survives him, as does his youngest brother, Frank.

Like most country lads, Leverett's early boyhood was passed in going to the district school during the short sessions and working on the farm during vacations. This continued until he was about ten years of age, when he entered the graded schools in the city of Lawrence, Massachusetts. He was always of a literary turn of mind, and even in his younger days stood well at the head of his class. It is remembered that he did not like the ordinary drudgery of farm work; but when anything definite had to be done he put in as hard work as a boy could.

At the breaking out of the war for the Union he was a member of the High School in Lawrence and belonged to a military company of boys which had been formed for the purposes of drill. On the return of the two Lawrence companies of the Sixth Massachusetts from their march through Baltimore, these boys turned out for the first time in uniform and under arms.

When President Lincoln issued a call for the first three-years troops Methuen immediately recruited, under command of Leverett's father, Captain Bradley, a full company, known as Company B, which was attached to the Fourteenth Regiment of Infantry rendezvousing at Fort Warren, in Boston Harbor, July 5, 1861. Captain Bradley thought it wise to take Leverett to wait on him, expecting then to be gone only ninety days. At that time Leverett was only fourteen, his fifteenth birthday being July 11. He attached himself to the company, acting as clerk.

The company left for the front in August, 1861, and on September 14 of the same year Leverett enlisted as a private in Company B of the regiment for three years, or during the war. He continued to act as company clerk. His younger brother Jerry enlisted as drummer-boy November 8.

During the remainder of 1861 the regiment was stationed in the forts around Washington, building and manning a line of works from Chain Bridge, opposite Georgetown, to Long Bridge, the lower end of Washington, and received the designation of the Fourteenth Massachusetts Heavy Artillery. In

1862, by orders from the War Department, the regiment was called the First Massachusetts Heavy Artillery, and was known by that name until the close of the war.

Susan Hinckley Bradley
1905

A Soldier-Boy's Letters

1862-1865

HEADQUARTERS HEAVY ARTILLERY,
14TH MASS. REGT., CO. B.
FORT ALBANY, *MARCH 5, 1862.*

Dear Mother and Brothers:

We fired a National Salute here yesterday in honor of the first anniversary of Lincoln's inauguration. It happened to be my detachment that fired it, so I can say I have helped fire a cannon 6 P.dr. brass. 20 guns were fired, then we limbered up and run into the Fort.

Well, how do you get along with the Geese? Jerry told me you were not going to keep any this year, but I am glad you are. Write me which ones you keep and ducks and hens, because I am a little anxious to know how things go long about the Bradley Farm.

We had a lively time here the other day. I was making out pay-rolls, but when the order came to fall in, I seized my old comrade [gun] and went down. We formed in line and the adjutant read the orders from McClellan to Division Generals; it was to be ready to march, how much we could carry and to keep 2 days Rations ahead, in case of emergency. We have had several other orders since which indicate a forward movement. I hope we shall go, fighting or not. Had a letter from Hull to-night. I have been making out papers to enable him to draw his pay in Massachusetts.

The Capt. has had a cold and does not feel very well. I have written a good long letter and I don't believe he will. Jerry is well and on guard as drummer. By our latest news we have possession of Columbus, that great place of the Rebels. I think our army of Kentucky has done the most so far. The Chaplin has got his wife out here and a Lieu't had his come to-night. We shall soon have a village.

We have men from Washington to work on the Fort, as the frost has caused the Ramparts to slide off into the ditch. We hear considerable said about going home; some say in a month, others a year and some three years. Don't make much difference to me.

As I know of nothing else to write, I will close.

Signed, Sealed in presence of

Leverett Bradley, Jr.

George, you may give my respects to the Gals and Boys about Pleasant Valley.

FORT ALBANY, VA., *MARCH 17, 1862.*

To the family in general:

The Army of the Potomac has moved and left us in the dark; there are not 100 men in the Regt. but what would like to go ahead.

McDowell's Division, which we once belonged to and then were put out of, and then into it again, and then off, is going to reinforce Burnside's. The Nelly Baker and Nantasket are down in the stream, with some 20 others, to take troops to some place. What do you think of our defeat at Manassas? We were not whipped, but we did not get a chance to fight. The talk is that McClellan will be superseded. I don't know it as a fact, but it is rumor. We are about played out writing out here. Like to get letters well enough but don't like to answer.

Here I shall close.

Lt-Brad Jr

P.S. Pleaseexcusethewritingwellyouknowitisbad don'tyouwellwhatdoYou think of Manassas?

Leverett Bradley Jr.

FORT ALBANY, VA., *MCH. 23, 1862.*

Dear Mother, Sister and Brothers:

We received a letter from home last night, and were glad you had sent your pictures. But I do not think that Mother's does her justice. She looks too thin and careworn: if so, I shall think it was on account of our leaving home, and the care falling on her has made her sick or unwell.

Frank has changed, it being 8 months since I have seen him. but he looks as if he would like to see us through his little eyes. He looks fat and healthy. And you had better believe we do, being so regular at our meals, and but few varieties which are best for our health. The weather has been rather better for the week past. Are having fine times after supper in games. Foot Ball, Base Ball, Cards, Checquers, Dancing and Singing.

Miss E. P. called up to see us the other night and took tea with us. She said that she was determined to eat a meal with the men at the Barracks, as that was what she came out for. The two companies to join the Regt. arrived here yesterday.

Caleb Saunders is a Lieu't in one. After religious services this forenoon the Col. was telling us about the reputation this Regiment has here, among the Big officers. About fifty thousand of the Army of the Potomac have left, they think to reinforce Burnside, and he is going to march on Richmond. A Regiment of Cavalry passed by here to-day; they looked finely. Send out my book-keeping by that boy. I have got a little cold and do not feel well enough to pick on the Old Banjo. The Capt. has gone up to see Capt. Wardwell at Fort Craig, about a mile from here.

I will close, perhaps to write a little to-morrow morn.

Yours, Leverett Bradley, Jr.

FORT BARNARD, VA., *APRIL 2, 1862.*

Dear Mother, Sister and Brothers:

You will see by this heading that we are still in Old Virginia.

The four companies which garrisoned this fort left this morning, and the Regt. Heavy Arty, like this one, started for Alexandria, to go down the river.

They left an immense pile of rubbish, bed-ticks, beds, stools, boards, stoves. I should judge they left at this place $150 worth of property. I am sitting before one of the stoves; it sends the heat out gay. I am writing on a book in my lap.

Another company of our Regt. came up to-day to help garrison the place.

I will give you a little idea where we are. We are three miles from Fort Albany; it mounts 10 Heavy guns. The Alexandria Rail Road runs about 150 rds. from us in the hollow; it is considered a place of much importance. The boy has not got here yet. Give my respects to the Boys and Gals on Pleasant Valley; mark you, I say gals. Well, to tell the truth, I have not seen one but Aunt Betsy. She shed a tear when she left, for Co. B.

Yours truly, Leverett Bradley, Jr

FORT BARNARD, VA., APR. 13, 1862.

There are few military movements around here. A regiment now and then goes up the road. I suppose they think the army is regulated and are now ready to fight. Mr. Wilson was here this afternoon and gave us a short discourse on strong drink and profane language. At dress parade he gave each man a tract. He is out here to take the money of the men home, if we ever get any. Now I must write out some passes and fill out a blank for discharge.

Yours truly, L. B., Jr.

FORT BARNARD, VA., *APRIL 16, 1862.*

Dear Mother:

Have just finished signing the pay-rolls; expect to get paid off to-morrow, but not certain.

I am very tired, but the captain says I must write ten lines.

I assure you, mother, I have not tasted anything which I have said I would not touch. No man can induce me to take whiskey, brandy, or gin, or anything of the kind. The captain had a present of some native wine which I have taken, but nothing stronger.

They have got a temperance society; but my word, if I give it. I will stick by.

To see so much drunkeness in camp is enough to make one despise the stuff even as medicine.

No news of importance from this quarter of the globe.

Good-night.   Yours truly,

Leverett Bradley, Jr.

FORT BARNARD, VA., *MAY 7, 1862.*

Dear Friends:

You will see we are still here and are likely to be till the end of the war.

You have got as much news as we have, probably, viz., Evacuation of Yorktown by the rebels and the taking of it by our forces. We had a large 10 in. Mortar brought here last night to practice with. We are going to fire Saturday. We have also one 30 lbs. rifled parrott gun which pointed at the enemy on Munson Hill last year, but never had a chance to pop at them. By the retreating of the rebels from Yorktown it has left us entirely out of danger; they were before some 75 miles away, but now 1:25 miles, so you see we were perfectly safe. Do not worry, because I do not think they will trouble us at present. The cars are passing now towards Leesburg from Alexandria; they have not run much lately.

Well, about this leaving home business. If you want to go, start, and we will follow (California or Mexico). We have got plenty of dogs and I am going to hunt for a living. Am going to get a horse, rifle and gun. pack up dogs and start, and I "reckon" you had better all do the same.

There is one lady in our camp, Capt. Shatswell's wife; she has been out since last winter —plucky. Also a negro woman who comes with milk every morning. Good-looking, but too dark complected to get too near to.

Yours,

L. B.

FORT BARNARD. VA., *MAY 14, 1862.*

Dear Mother:

We have had great news for the week past, but are a little anxious about Halleck; afraid he will be whipped and that will be a stunner. Norfolk has been taken. You will have heard of it before this reaches you; however, it is good news. I can scarcely hear myself think, the drums are beating so like the old Harry.

Roll-call. Bed-time.

TUESDAY MORNING, 6 A.M.

Just answered to the roll-call and now can write a line. We had mortar firing the other day. The shell can be seen in the air; it goes to an immense height and then comes down on the object smash. The shell weighs 91 lbs.

It would be a good thing if a fellow had got to die, to have it drive him in; but he would want it taken off afterwards, because it would make a fellow's head ache.

Yours,

L. Bradley, Jr.

FORT BARNARD, VA., JULY 2, 1862.

Dear Mother, Sister and Brothers:

It is a cold chilly night and has been all day, for this date. I am crowding as close to the stove as I can sit, in order to keep up animal heat outwardly. I have got acquainted with a farmer's son about a quarter of a mile from here. The Capt. is well acquainted with the man; he owns a large amount of property around here. The fort is built on his ground. They are a fine family. We go off together Sundays, he having to work other days. He has got two horses under his care; was cutting hay yesterday. As I was going to say, we went off Sunday and visited all the place; he knows all about here and of course knows the girls. I ate supper with them the other night, so you see I am all hunk. Going to get acquainted with some rich young lady, marry and settle down. I suppose you think I am going to work rather early. Well, count it we are Soldiers. Isn't it a great thing to be a Soldier!

We don't get much war news; expect to hear soon that McClellan is in Richmond. I am going to try to go to a picnic 4th of July. I have finished the muster rolls which I have to make out every two months. Here I must close, or at least try to! Love to all.

Yours truly,

Leverett Bradley, Jr.

P. S. I don't think much of this letter, but could not think of anything to write.

[On July 11 he had his sixteenth birthday. Ed.]

FORT BARNARD, VA., *JULY 17, 1862.*

Dear Mother, Sister and Brothers:

It is quite a long time since I last wrote. Have had a spell of sickness. I had a fever, then the shakes, which are very comfortable(!) to have on one.

I had to take Quinine for the first time and the taste of it was in my mouth two days after; it loosened every tooth in my head. War news not very exciting. A string of over two hundred teams passed up by here day before yesterday; they are going to help move Pope's army, but it will take some time to find it.

It has been hot; sweat runs off in streams. George Frye is well. Here I will close and give the Capt. room to write.

Yours,

L. B., Jr.

FORT BARNARD, VA., *AUG. 7, 1862.*

Dear Mother:

My health is improving rapidly, but still they say I look like a ghost. Yesterday there was a large review (that is, for round here) at Fort Ward.

I did not go in the ranks, but Jere came along from Arlington House, so I went along with him. It was terribly hot; but I stood it as well as the ones who are full of health. Reviewing officers were Abraham Lincoln, Gen's. Whipple and Sturgis. He looked as if he had a great deal on his mind (A. L.), dressed very plain; reminded me of old Scripture look in his face. Every fort fired a salute. I expected to see Gen. Hallek, but I was disappointed, because I went almost on purpose to see him. He was not present. How does that order for the draft take hold of the men north? It makes the boys feel good that they have got to come. The general health of the Regt. is good; but they are trying to kill the men, drilling in the hot sun six hours a day. Mother said she did not care for long letters, so I will close.

Love to all. Yours truly,

L. B.. Jr.

[written in pencil]

IN CAMP AT CLOUD'S MILLS, VA., *AUG. 28, 1862.*

Dear Mother:

Received yours to-night all right. You will see by this that we are not at Fort Barnard as usual. There has been a great deal of maneuvering around here lately about where to move and it has finally come to us; we have expected it for some time. We have had a great time moving; did it today, about four miles from former place and on the R.R. to Mannassas. Pope has been down on 20 miles; and reinforcements are going out by thousands and right by our sides some orders were to go on; but on account of ammunition we had to encamp here for tonight. Don't know but we shall go in ten minutes, and perhaps not till morning. Jere and myself are in a small tent by ourselves; we are experiencing camp life. Had no dinner and nothing but a cup of coffee for supper and do not expect anything again for two days; we can not get hold of any bread, having none for two weeks back. It is now about 8.30 p.m. Batteries and other Regts. going with us are on the move here to report. Cavallery also. We got rifles in last night and had to go 3 miles to get them. I have a nice one. I slept well, you better believe, last night; wore the skin off my hip bone laying on the soft side of a plank (knotty); got a softer one tonight (the ground). Don't be scared, for it is fun for us and will try to stick it out to the last. We may be 100 miles from here tomorrow. Write as usual, and if we get it, all right, and if not, the same. We will write as much as we can and often; but let me tell you again do not be worried because it does no good and makes us feel bad.

The drummer boy is well and looking on the scene. We are both lying on the ground. Nothing more to write; do not know if this will reach you. Capt will write in the morning, if we do not move before.

Don't worry about us!   Yours truly,

Leverett Bradley, Jr.

FORT CORCORAN, VA., *AUG. 23, 1862.*

Dear Mother:

Rec'd yours. We have had a tramp since writing last. Our orders came last Tuesday night to report to Gen. Sturgis at Warrenton; took up the line of march at 9 o'clock, marched seven miles that night and halted about 12 o'clk. to rest our wearied limbs in a field. Slept well; started early next morning and went two miles and halted to wash up and eat. While there, a report came that the 2nd New York (H. A.) in our brigade was all cut up, also that a battery had been taken from us. We then started on a forced march. We soon met the supply trains coming back and we marched by a train ten miles long, 1000 horses, 1500 cattle. We had got just the other side of Fairfax, about 2 miles, when at the top of a hill, in the woods, the remaining two pieces of the battery and some cavalry came rushing by, telling us the enemy were coming and for us to look out for ourselves. We jumped for the woods and waited, but they did not come; we then formed in line of battle about a mile long in the woods and waited. Co. B. was moved to the right, the hardest position, and a squad of men taken way out into the woods to look out for our flank, myself with them; this was the dangerous post, guarding a road they would pass in coming on us. This happened at 2 o'clk. We waited for them, but they did not come. The next morning, soon after getting up, we heard three shots. We jumped (our little squad) and concealed ourselves and waited; but it proved to be our pickets firing at each other. One of Co. A got shot through both legs; not hurt much. Soon after the Dr. and asst. Surgeon, steward and five others, with 2 teams and an ambulance, went back to Fairfax to make a hospital; while there, 500 Cavalry rushed on them and took all prisoners, but released the Drs. and kept the rest and teams and 8 horses, so you see the enemy had got behind us and we were in a fix. It was Lee of the cavalry and he sent a note to Col. Greene and to Gen. Sturgis; he was in the class of the Col. The Col. knew that it was not best for us to stop long, but to retreat back to Cloud's Mills. We had considerable to look after, our teams and stores; we got ready to go, when we were sent back to old place again. Things looked rather dubious; soon we heard the roll. We all jumped to our guns ready for them; the picket came in and said that cavalry were coming. Of course we expected Rebel. I expected to get shot; hid myself in the bushes and waited, but they proved to be some cavalry come out to reinforce us, so we were all right; we sent them out scouting. They were gone an hour; they reported some 5000 rebels four miles from us, so we started as soon as possible. First went cavalry, next a battalion of our Regt., then all our wagons and 2 cannon, next two Battalions of our Regt., A. C's. rear guard and some cavalry behind. We saw about 50 of them on the edge of the woods when we started, but they did not molest us; we kept up marching 18 miles from 7 o'clk. till 12 at night, resting only 3 times. They followed us until we came within 4 miles of Cloud's Mills. Soon after, Col. Greene was ordered to report to McClellan, who ordered us into these forts. The report now is, that Jackson has surrendered; there was heavy fighting off there yesterday; heard the cannon plainly. All well. Love to all.

L. B., Jr.

We shall probably stay here now and not be moved off, because some one wants us ! We are nearer Washington but farther up, opposite Georgetown. Very fine view.

FORT CRAIG, VA., *SEPT. 10, 1862.*

Dear Mother:

Yours received all right. The rebels are driving the union army back by the mile. Reports say that Jackson is invading Penn. Glad of it; it will serve to raise the men to a sense of duty. The boys have begun already to come down on the ($300) three hundred dollar men. It gets them a little snappish; but they can do nothing for themselves. I don't know but we shall have a chance to come home, that is if Jackson is going to be good enough to drive us the right way and back there. He brags now of going just where he wants to; he always has, why can't he now just as well as then? Time will show. The Captain's health is good, also mine; Jere's improving as fast as he declined. I would like to go north and "hiper" you fellows up once, and ask you what you are at. Afraid to go to war; but will sell your lives for $300. Well you spoke about short ones — letters, I mean. This is short and sweet. George B. and George Frye are well. Love to all.

Am yours truly,

Leverett Bradley, Jr.

Excuse writing, as we have but few conveniences. Amen.

FORT CRAIG, VA., *OCT. 15, 1862.*

Dear Family:

The men suffer very much from cold, having had no blankets since the advance, only what they could pick up, and nothing but the soft side of a board to sleep on; but I sleep as well as at home, having nearly all the conveniences of that place.

You think I had better "stop in camp than go out roaming around the country" Well the fact is, a fellow gets tired of laying round, and another reason is, I want to see the country; it is different from that in Mass., being hills and valleys everywhere. I should like to go to a meeting where there is some kind of a man going to speak; have not heard one since being out here and fear that I am no better on account of it, although but little good our Chaplain would or could do. As for the country being ruined, I think it will get along as well as usual for some time to come. Our men can fight as well as the southerners; but I'm better. They have got good fighting blood and are as smart as we; but it is supposed we outnumber them; still, don't know. They have held their own with us so far and should not be surprised if they did to the end. The Capt. has got his papers at last. Shall not expect a box, now the Capt. has gone, till Thanksgiving.

I suppose Frank has got to be quite an old man by this time and thinks he is boss.

About those photographs; we can get fine ones taken over in the city. Which would you rather have, the whole body or the bust? I think the latter for me, as they say I am a tall gawky looking fellow. The report here is now that we have got to go to California; that there is a large fleet off that coast and they want us out there. I should like to go as I could get out free of cost. Do you suppose you could get any pay from the state, on Jere and myself.' Seems as though you might, other families do. I will draw up something if you think best and get Lt. H. to sign it and see if that will do. Write if you think best or not. The old members of Co. B are determined that if they get home they will draw a town meeting and vote to give us bounty ($300) and I have no doubt they 'd get the vote.

Much love to all. Give respects to all inquiring friends.

Yours, L. B., Jr.

Oct. 16.

I am just out of bed and am going to add a few lines. The new troops are drilling and they have to drill like good ones too. Sitting here at the door of the tent, I get a view of the Potomac. If the Capt. should go home, if you look in his trunk and get the picture of a young lady, keep it for me. It is a Virginia lass.

[Captain Bradley returned home in October, 1862. Leverett had been clerk of the company for nearly a year, and he had shown great ability for taking pains and accuracy. He learned to write very evenly and picked up knowledge at every turn. The clear perception for which he was noted in after-life can be traced here. The discipline in a camp where petty jealousies and quarrels filled the leisure hours consisted in keeping free from them and rising to every opportunity for responsibility. He also developed his ability to keep his temper and learned to hold his tongue. He was very thoughtful of the family at home, and felt the care of his brother Jere, the drummer-boy, who at this time was fourteen. Leverett was sixteen. The restricted circumstances of the family during the war made him conscientious about self-support. Ed.]

Oct. 29, 1862.

To the family at home:

How would you like me to get in the navy? You know I spoke of it before I left home and it has. been in my head ever since, 1st for, and then against it. I don't know as I could; but would try hard. I think you could do all you could there, and I, here; but I would not do it against your wish. Mr. G. is one of them to get a chance at and I didn't know but what the Capt. and he could talk and I would see Asst. Secretary Fox, of the Navy here. It is the only service that has done anything since the war. I don't know as I could get out of the army, into it; but think I could. I, perhaps, could pass no kind of an examination; but I think I could get very good recommendations. Now don't say "pooh," but just think it over and see what you think of it. It is the place to bring up a boy anyway. There are land services and sea services. Now, please ponder and weigh the subject well and give only your opinion. You may think I have changed that "California" note; but by this means I could stand a better sight.

SUNRISE.

The beautiful morning sun is just peeping into my tent quite cheerily. It was not very cold last night and I slept like a good one. Have answered roll-call and built a fire and now can write. Can Frank go through the sword exercise.

I hope you will meet with success in your great speech to be made shortly. Have everything on your tongue's end that you are going to say and then let them have it; but I don't know as I can give you any advice.

[He was sixteen, writing to his father. Ed.]

FORT CRAIG, VA., *Nov. 19, 1862.*

Dear family:

I am getting better day by day, but by what the boys say, am rather thin. They want to know what deed they have done, that a ghost should appear before them. I go by the name of Hamlet's ghost; but I expect soon to get my old flesh on again. I am feeling first rate. The butter tastes first rate; I eat toasted bread and butter. I think it quite a relish to get hold of such stuff right along. Will do as you direct about money matters; if I can't get over to the city myself I'll send by the sutler. I think he can be trusted. Those shirts are very comfortable. I had but one the afternoon they came, and I had a bath and a change of clothes. Jere is on guard and cannot write. They have got so they put drummers on guard, the same as at Barnard; but he does not stop on all night, that is one good thing. We never have had so much sickness before. Burnside is doing a big thing, and if he don't go through with it he will get kicked out, and receive no mercy from

the public at large and some one else will come in. "O—He is the man. He is the man." Then they will kick him out, and that is the way it will go. I am tired, as you will see by my waiting.

From Lev.

Fort Craig, Va., *Dec. 21, 1862.*

Dear Family:

Glad to hear of your good health. We are in the same condition. It has been terribly cold weather for us.

The war news is of but little importance. The report is, we are to have a new cabinet, and that Seward has resigned. The men throughout the army are getting discouraged, and men from Fredericksburg say if officers were to try their best to lead them into another fight on the same ground the men would not follow. It was a perfect butchery of our men. Fremont (some think) will get either Sec. of War or command of the army. Report this morning was Halleck had resigned.

Don't sell old Sam *[a dog]* unless you get a good price for him, because you know he is mine.

Later.

We have rec'd orders to go to Harper's Ferry to-morrow and Jere had to get drum head. We shall carry most everything; will send you a box of extra clothing, pay at that end. I am packing up as fast as I can. The boys feel first rate; will write if there is anything new.

L. B., Jr.

Maryland Heights, *Dec, 1862.*

Dear Friends:

Have not rec'd your letter yet. We arrived here after an all night's ride in the cars and then had to tramp this mountain. We are 1100 ft. above the river and it is cold all the time. We have to go a mile and | to get up here and it is a steep and rocky path. We have 7 guns, 5 Boat Howitzers and 12 Pdr Field guns. There are two beautiful valleys, one on each side of us, named Pleasant Valley and Valley of the Potomac. The Shenandoah river comes in here. We have a fine view of

Harper's Ferry, but it is mostly deserted except by sutlers. The Rebs show themselves once in a while; they are guerillas of the Hampton's League.

We are alone here on the mountain, the other Co's are further down. We have a great job to get water; have to go a mile down and then three can get only enough for coffee. Start half rations twice a day. It is rather tough; but what is the use of being a soldier if you aren't one. There are a lot of Rebs buried outside the battery, killed in the fight. We are both well. Wish I could have those things in G's box. Love to all.

Lev.

MARYLAND HEIGHTS, *Dec. 28, 1862.*

Dear Family:

We have no letter from you. We are situated on the highest point of the Blue Range. Can see a distance of 40 miles in the valley of Virginia, and mountains some 75 miles distant. To the south west, on the opposite side of the river, is the village of Charlestown, where John Brown was hung, some 12 miles from here. To the N. W. is Martinsburg, 50 miles. It is a beautiful sight to see, worth coming for. Can see the valley of the Shenandoah for 15 miles, so notorious for the retreats and advances of the two armies of Gen. Banks and Jackson. There was a great commotion here, the other night, caused by a dispatch from the two Gens, at Winchester that the enemy was coming and that they would fall back on Harper's Ferry. But they haven't come yet. The men are building barracks 24 in. thick. The detachment of Company H left two, which they had built for themselves. From the direction the rebels came, when they took the place, are lots of what might be called graves, with toes and hands out of the ground. The boys get bones and buttons and such things as relics. We have had a hard time of it so far; but no cause to grumble. Hard work to get food or water up the mountain. It takes five mules to bring a half load of water and that takes half a day. We are trying to get a pack mule to bring water. They are going to have a signal station. They are signaling now to a point of rocks 12 miles down the river, the place where the rebs crossed at the battle of Antietam. Capt., I will ask if once a week won't do to write long letters? Time flies faster up here; we are above the clouds a good part of the time.

I expect muster rolls to-day, but have nothing but an old box to make them out on. I am writing now on a cigar-box cover on my lap.

[His writing and spelling had taken a great jump in a few weeks, showing unconscious control and a high standard in these respects. Ed.]

MD. HEIGHTS, JAN. 25, 1863.

Dear Family:

Have written a note to Lizzie *[his sister]*. She says her school is "behaving in behavior." We stop in No. 9 tent; it is stockaded and in rear of barracks; the women have our shanty.

FEB. 1.

We were all paid up Thursday for four months. I shall send the money by Adams express. I have collected all in the Co. but P. and G—n's. I think I can get G—n's before I send money; P's is doubtful. Shall send Geo. Bricket's with mine. We had a terrible storm; here on the Mountain the snow is two feet deep and it blows. M. was promoted to Corpl. yesterday. S. was broke. The boys are very indignant about it; you know he did not come out until last Sept. We have got so we have a row every day. Capt. has some one to the wheel every night; he has got the rough ones down on him. Co. sent home $1709 yesterday and paid debts for 6 months. I went down to the Naval battery and collected two bills there. There is a report that we are to move. Shall send our money on Tuesday, so look out for it. If we happen to move shall wait. Much love to all from

Lev., Jr.

BOAT HOWITZER BATTERY, MD. HEIGHTS,

Feb. 8, 1863.

Dear Mother and Father:

    Yours found us all well. I started the money last Wednesday $196 (one hundred and ninety six). George Bricket sent $32 which you will please deliver to uncle Frank; he paid me for sending it. It cost $1.50 for sending it; kept $1 out and paid the rest from my own. I shall keep dunning for the rest of those notes till I get it. Should not be surprised if we got paid again soon. The boys have all paid up their bills well. H. deserted, has not been heard from since pay day; most likely will keep clear and not get caught. We have an order to stop the Artillery practice and we have got a shelf fixed so we can take Shell of all kinds to pieces. There is an examination of Sergt's for promotion; it is an order from Col. S. He will recommend them to Gov. Andrew. An Ex Capt. D. is at the Hooks on a spree and some of the boys go down and have one with him. There is a time coming when the men of Co. B will have a chance to speak their thoughts and minds and they will do it. The men still think a great deal of Capt. Bradley, or, as they call him, " Snap it up." Your name is spoken a great many times a day, and many are the wishes that you were commander now. I may stand a chance yet. My duty is much harder than at Craig, on account of commanding the post. Have to make out returns of ammunition every Monday morning, &c.
  Much love to all.

Leverett, Jr.

Md. Heights, *Feb. 22, 1863.*

Dear Family:

Yours found us all well. This is the anniversary of the birth of Geo. Washington. We had an order yesterday to hold divine service at 10 o'clk A.M. together with a dress parade; but we had a severe snow storm last night and it has snowed ever since, the hardest we have had. Sergt. R. applied for a furlough; but the Major refused to forward it, on the ground that several had received them and have not been heard from since. T. is trying to get one; went over to see the Gen'l yesterday, but got no definite answer. Capt.— has not been heard from since keeping a hotel! The news seems to be a little more encouraging; we must have a defeat or victory at Vicksburg and along the Charleston coast. The papers speak of English and French mediation in our affairs, but I don't know as it will amount to anything. Last night they spoke of the French Army in Mexico; they have had several defeats and I guess they will have to work hard to get a good substantial position any where in Mexico. The boys say that Capt. Bradley and Genl. McClellan are their men. What do they think of the way Gov. Andrew used Genl. McClellan on his late visit to Massachusetts? The boys don't have a very good opinion of his doings; in fact he is not liked amongst the troops. Now I will give Mother a little news, or rather answer some of her kind questions. I kept money enough to pay up old bills and a little on hand. We both kept $5 a piece; you see Jere only draws $12 a month to my $13. We fare as well as can be expected; in fact we have all we can eat and more too. Draw fresh beef and no salt or corned, keep twelve days rations ahead. To give you an idea of what we have (and you must judge the cooking; but we think it good, Cyrus Messer is cook now). Well first, we have coffee. Bread, fresh beef, with some that we salt. Bread of the best quality, potatoes, dried apples and molasses, and a soup twice a week; have vinegar, salt &c.. as much as we want. I should like to write to all of my relations; but some times I don't feel like answering

letters and then it stops. I hope I shall be able to correspond with Home, as I may well call it, once a week.
Love to all.

Leverett Bradley, Jr.

MD. HEIGHTS, *MARCH 8, 1863.*

Dear Father:

Yours reed. Am sorry to hear that you are so afflicted with rheumatism, it must come hard to you, as you have always been so healthy. There are only two sergt's called from each company. They were examined, and a hard ex', it w as. I assure you there is a feeling for you here; there is scarcely a day goes by but what I hear your name spoken of in good terms. The non-commissioned officers recite once a week from the red book on artillery. They are going into the thing scientiffically; have bought several useful books on artillery and take hold of it with energy. I do not get lessons, but I am in the room when they recite and gather considerable information. I took a tramp with several of the boys to Solomon's Gap, 5 miles out on the ridge; it is cut through the mountain; could see plainly where the battle of South Mt. was fought, it is about 12 miles from here. Would it pay for me to have a firkin of butter come out here? I will leave it all to you; butter is 35 cts. a lb. here and scarce at that. If it will pay ship it along, as there are plenty of chances to dispose of it. The Lieut, assigned to the Co. has not arrived yet. There are many reports going here; one is that we are going back to Fort Warren! Very respectfully yours,

L. Bradley, Jr.

MD. HEIGHTS, *MARCH 25, 1863.*

Dear Friends:

Glad to hear the Capt. is improving. We are well. Affairs are the same as the other day. The Lieuts. are still under arrest; some are at the naval guard house, took them out of the magazine on account of their health.

The signal Officer at this post received a dispatch from Martinsburg that we have Vicksburg in our possession, it has not got out yet. Tonight's paper had no news, but the report is they are evacuating Vicksburg and are going to throw their whole force on Rosecrans; Burnside is at Cincinnati on his way to the army of the south west. I do hope that we shall be able to give them a severe whipping all round before long. It is about time something was done. I want you to send me two boxes of salt mackerel A. no 1. I can get ten cents a piece for them by keeping them till pay day-I am sure if you will get them for me, that I can get out whole with a little over. I shall expect all the butter you can send, as we need it very much, having nothing to eat but our bread, coffee and beef. " I must have my butter! "What do you think the prospect is of our getting home .Of course you know it can not be till the war is over. The general opinion is that six months will see all the fighting over. One thing more, we must not give them peace, unless honorable to our arms; there must be no squeezing out place, keep them until they submit to our terms. The end greatly depends upon our success at Vicksburg, port Hudson, and Charleston. If we whip them at these places I think Joe Hooker will start them and will drive them till they get some thing very strong to hide behind. About influence, I don't urge my case hard, but just mention the thing, and if any thing should turn up, you might put it to use in my case, as I am in the army. I think not to use any braggadocio, that I am as capable as a great many others. Jere will write next Sunday. Much love to all.

Yours &c.L. Bradley, Jr.

BOAT HOWITZER BATTERY, MD. HEIGHTS,

APRIL 5, 1863.

Dear Friends:

I received three letters and a box. The major has got up a new signal code for the benefit of the officers; each one knowing them, they talk with the other batteries. I see by the paper that McClellan has made his report of his campaign, it will be out next week. The voice of the army is still for him, and no wonder, in his report he gives all the praise to the men. He says that " to the calm judgment of history he leaves the task of pronouncing on the movement, confident that its verdict will be, that no such difficult one was ever more successfully executed. That no army ever fought more heroically, repeatedly, and successfully against such odds, that no men of any race, ever displayed greater discipline, endurance, patience and cheerfulness under such hardships." No wonder that the soldier's heart clings to him. for the reason that he is right, but has been shamefully abused.

Gen'l. Morris, formerly Col. of the N. Y. 6. Heavy Artillery, has command of us now, or rather we are in his brigade. All of his staff officers are from his regiment and he does not look with much respect on this battalion. Major R. will not stand much from him; they have only been in the service since last Oct. They have the idea that they can whip the world. It really seems as if we were never going to move.

I hope they will put the conscription act in force soon. I have no doubt some men north would as leave let the south have all they want rather than come out here. What kind of men do you call them? They think a great deal of their Country! If you have an opportunity, get the Adjutant general of Massachusetts's report for 1862, it is a good thing. News from Fort Albany is big, I forgot to write it before. Major W. is a 2nd Lieut in the N. Y. 2nd H. A. H. D. is being court martialled for drunkenness. Capt's C. and A. have resigned and also Lt. S. Col. W. has preferred charges against Col. C. Grand chance for promotion, which there always has been in this regt, but there is no chance for poor W.

From Lev.

Md. Heights, Apr. 20, 1863.

Dear Father:

I hope this will find you improving in health. As soon as R. returned here the first questions were, if he went to see the old Captain? We had a grand inspection here yesterday by Genl. Barry, Chief of artillery for the army; he complimented us on our good looks, i.e. as soldiers. I was complimented by Major R. for the neatness of an inventory of Ordanance and ordanance stores of this post, which I had to make out. The Major has no clerk now; he asked the Capt. for me but I don't know what answer he gave. I shall keep still and if I think it is for my interest to take it, shall do so. You know I have a good position now and move or no move, I shall probably have it unless some other thing interferes. As it is now Adj. Hervey has asked the Capt. if I cant go down and help him after I have made out the muster rolls, as he has more than he can attend to on account of the returns. For the last two days it has rained and the Barracks being leaky we spoke of moving our clothes out to dry! I forgot in my last to answer a few questions. I am 5 ft. 10 in. high. Don't know my weight. Now you that have not seen me since I left home, don't go to imagining a great big fellow, because it ain't so; but there is consolation in the fact that I have got a few years to thicken up in; but you can imagine a good looking fellow! I wish you could see the scenery, the late rains have changed the grass from a deadly color to a green. B. M. is at Fort Albany, having returned on account of the president's proclamation to deserters. We have had five desert since we have been up here, one of Methuen's $300 men; he had nearly $50 of G. F—'s . This makes 3 of that stamp. Methuen has lost so much of recruits. Love to all. I remain, Yours &c.,

L. Bradley, Jr.

Md. Heights, May 10, 1863.

Dear Family:

Glad to hear that the Capt. is improving. The rumor here is that Richmond is taken. It was nearly "taps" last night and I was preparing to turn in, when the cry was to fall in. I dressed immediately and went out. The Lieut, read a letter from Major R. to the effect that Keyes had taken Richmond. I can assure you there was some tall cheering. It further stated that extras were being issued in Phil'a, N. Y. and Boston and that the people were perfectly crazy with excitement; but he also says, don't think too much of it, it may need conformation. The dispatch was from Head Quarters at Baltimore to Genl. Kelly, and it doesn't seem possible that they would send it unless they were very confident it was so. If you have got the news there and are making such a time over it, such as firing salutes &c. &c. and then it should turn out to be a hoax, what a feeling of despondency would invade the heart of every true soldier and Avorse than that, what would be the feelings of the people of the whole north! I do hope and pray that it is taken, and if so, see the position Lee's army is in; it has no chance of escape; there is also a rumor that Vicksburg is taken by the combined forces of Genl. Grant and Rear Admiral Porter; this does not look so promising as the other, considering the relative positions of the two forces; but still I hope it may be so. I see the conscription act is going into effect soon. It makes the boys delighted, because they want to see some of those rabid men in Methuen. Just been up on the parapet of the fort signaling to the 30 Prd Battery; on account of the sun, can only make out "good news." I hope so, the Capt. is going down to see. I wish you were here to see the sight we see every day and that is, the different valleys visible in all parts from here; the grass has put on his coat and the trees have begun to bud. To speak plainly, it is the most beautiful scenery I ever looked on. The Capt. has got back; the news is confirmed of the taking of Richmond with 70 cannon.

Much love to all from   Lev.

Md. Heights, May 24, 1863.

Dear Friends:

Yours found us all well. Was sorry to hear that Aunt D. was so near her end; but hers has been a life of sickness. We might say her last moments on earth would be the happiest she ever enjoyed for years. But to change the topic to the great cry of the nation, when is the war to be settled. I must say the matters look pretty blue. We must gain a victory soon, in some quarter and a great victory at that. If the papers speak the truth, the feelings of the people North are a little disloyal; I don't mean in Mass., but more particularly the "Empire State," especially on the Vallandigham case. He is a traitor and why not give him his dues? I see that he was not to be sent to Fort Warren but through our lines to the south. I hope Gov. Seymour will soon follow him; he certainly does no good to our cause, but on the contrary a great deal of harm. The weather has been very hot, but if there is a breeze we get it. It is beginning to get hard on us again, to have to go half way down the mountain for water, and if we don't have rain soon, shall have to go to the foot. It is not very pleasant crawling up the mountain with a few canteens and a scorching sun sending its burning rays on to the back. Lieut. H. has returned to Co. H for duty; while here he won the enthusiasm of the men; if the men did not know the drill, he would take hold and show them and not damn them. The feelings of the Co. are worse than they have ever been before. I have no doubt if they had a leader to carry out any thing, some change might take place in the Company. There are fears that Harper's Ferry will be attacked. The rebs have shown themselves rather plucky lately. I wish you would send me out my Spanish book; we are having a small class in the barracks I stop in. Have got one man that can speak well. I have some one ask me every day how you are and if I think you will come out here this summer. What do you think of it? I remain, Your obt. servant,

L. B., Jr.

MD. HEIGHTS, JUNE 14, 1863.

Dear Family:

Yours of Sunday found us all well. I made a tour to Antietam last week; I hired a horse for a $1.00, rode about 30 miles, was tired enough when I got back. There were four of us, had a fine time. Visited all the places of interest; but the farmers have cleared up the grounds and it does not look as if a great battle had been fought there. I got but few relics. The Capt. is heading a paper to get Jere a bugle. Affairs are progressing in Co. B as usual, that is every one is dissatisfied. Co. I has gone to Winchester to garrison there. A dispatch came yesterday that the Rebs were making a raid up this way and to have all ready and manned for an emergency. When last heard from they were at Berryville on the Shenandoah river and working this way. Genl. Imbroke had command. We lost several officers and men. Some one has come up from the Ferry and says citizens are coming in from Martinsburg and reporting the rebels 10000 strong within a mile of that place; probably the number is exaggerated. We have now five companies on the hill. They do picket duty around the hill, front of the battery.

MONDAY MORNING.

We were turned out again about 12 m. last night with a report that the rebs were at Martinsburg and working this way. We saw a big engagement about 10 miles from here, saw the flash of the guns plain. Rumors say it was Milroy's forces and that they have been beaten. The Hook is full of women and children from the country, 40 trains came down from the valley yesterday. Saw a train of cars on fire last night. We may have a small engagement before the week is out.

From Lev.

MD. HEIGHTS, *JUNE 24, 1863.*

Dear Family:

I have no doubt you have felt a little anxiety for our welfare; we are safe and sound as ever, but pretty well surrounded. We have a fine view of the enemy, they are in strong force all through the valley; rumors say that Genl. Hooker is after them; he has crossed part of their force to the Md. side. A signal corps came with very large glasses to take observations. I have had some fine views at them. We have strengthened our fortifications greatly, working night and day, consequently a great deal of excitement. I should have written before, but had no chance to send. I hope this will reach you. I have had no letters as yet, trains do not run at all; an officer is going to the Relay house and I send by him. The whole Co. is well and in good spirits.

Much love to all from   Lev.

[On the advance of Lee's army up the valley, they were engaged at the battle of Winchester and the evacuation of Harper's Ferry, falling back with the main army to Frederick City. Ed.]

[Written in pencil.]

IN THE FIELD, FREDERICK JUNCTION, MD.,

JULY 4, 1863, 1.30 P.M.

Dear Family:

Have just rec'd yours of June 21. I have been unable to write before as I, or rather all of us, have been in the move. Orders came a week ago today for the evacuation of Harper's Ferry and the destruction of all the ordinance stores from Genl. Hooker, who was there; but before we set to work, the order was countermanded by Genl. Halleck. But orders came in earnest on Monday; all the guns were removed but the old ones and the 100 pdr., which were destroyed. The ammunition was all destroyed. There was an explosion at the South 30 pdr. Battery, some of the green 8th N. Y. H. A. went in with axes, striking Cap shell and exploding the pile; some five or six were killed. Started for the Hook about 1 o'clk on the 30th; worked all the afternoon and night loading guns on to canal boats, raining all the time, wetting the boys to the skin; started from Sandy Hook on the 1st of July, about 8 o'clk, for fire brick. Our battalion has to do this work alone. Two brigades were hours ahead of us and one to start 12 hours after. Frederick is about 20 miles from Sandy Hook. It was very muddy, and the boys were wet through; about noon the sun came out terribly hot and it sickened some of the boys. Mind you, we had started with but little, but by this time had thrown every thing away. I saved nothing but what was on my back and a sulphur Blanket, lost every thing else. Encamped about 7 miles from Frederick and stopped over night, got there next morning, stopped till noon and then started for here, 3 miles, and here we all are, on the banks of the Monocacy river at the junction.

We are all well; will write Sunday.

Lev.

BETWEEN HAGERSTOWN AND FREDERICK JUNCTION,

JULY 11, 1863.

Dear Family:

So far we have received your letters in due time. We are right on the tramp. My last letter I left off rather suddenly; I had no intention of sending it in that mail, but the boy came round and said, mail was going. We started from F. June, on the 7th at 5 p.m., marched through Fred'k and out on the Middletown pike, about 9 miles and turned in for the night. (A band has just struck up Hail Columbia, two yards from here; it stirs me so, I can hardly write!) Have been on the road ever since and are at last at destination. Reserve artillery corps, commanded by Genl. Tyler. We are now in the Fort, are going to have some guns; we expected we should have to go in as infantry. If you will get a map, showing the roads in Maryland and Virginia, I will every time I write, show the route which may be interesting to you; it is very probable we, of this battalion, shall keep with the army of the Potomac the rest of the time. On the way here, we passed where the cavalry passed last Thursday; a great many had horses in the woods and along the road we could see where shot had struck. We are now beginning to see a little service, nothing but hard tack, pork and coffee, which we have to cook ourselves, but still I like it. In fact I like the whole thing. I think I shall fat up on it. Being tough, will eat, drink and sleep together. We have had a chance to see a great deal of the old Army, some regiments have but about 40 men; one Co. went into the fight with 33 men, 27 were shot dead on the spot. Some Regts. have been consolidated five times and have now but about 200 men, it is awful to think of. There were a great many killed on both sides, in the last battle. We are trying our best to catch Johnny Reb. Don't know as we shall .succeed. Should not be surprised if there was a great battle tomorrow, you know Sundays are the days for big fights. The boys are feeling well, but have no desire to be in a fight but would like to see one. Have seen any quantity of the Johnnies lately, not less than 2000 taken prisoner since the last fight. I wish you could see them, they don't look as if they belonged to the American Continent; they have a very peculiar look. All of the boys had quite a talk with them, they talk better than they look. I am today the same boy L. B. Jr.; but a few years older than when I left, I am 17 today. The regiment has now been in the service over two years, will soon be nine months more. If you see uncle Frank tell him that George and the rest are well. We dont have much of a chance to write but certainly will once a week. Direct yours to the same as ever, with the exception of the place Washington, D. C. That is the place. Jere is well and sends his love. Much love to all from

Leverett.

[During the Gettysburg campaign a large number of Company B were detached from the regiment and placed in the light batteries of the regular army to make up the losses caused by this severe campaign. Ed.]

FORT DUNCAN, MD., *JULY 27, 1863*.

Dear Family:

We have received no letters since we were at Fred. June. We have been on the tramp ever since and by several counter marches we are at length in old Maryland again, on the hill that Co. C garrisoned last winter. I should have written before, but have been unwell and have been so on the whole tramp; but I have made out to keep with the Co. all the time. We have been with the "Artillery Reserve" until last week, when we received orders to report to the Comd'g officer of Harper's Ferry. We were at the time at a small village called Unionsville in Va. about 29 miles from Harper's Ferry; we started at 7.30 a.m. and made 6 rests until we reached Berlin, this side of the river, 23 miles distant from Unionsville. The doctor had something: to say on the tramp. The major was going to put us through to B. without any thing to eat, except hard tack which we carry in our haversacks; but the Dr. said he must stop and let us make some coffee; of course the Major obeyed. We reached B. at 8 p.m., where we took mother earth for a couch with a rubber blanket under and a woolen over; of course slept sound, woke in the morning rather stiff; during the whole tramp did not stop in one place but twice, only for a day; we have got so now we can stand quite a tramp, they say we look like "old soldiers." I have nothing but what I have on my back, except rubber and wool blankets. We were for a while all split up into different batteries in the "Reserve Artillery." George Bricket was detailed into the 5th Regular. It left us at Berlin, was put on the cars and started for X. Y. to help put down the riot, seventeen others are in the same battery; those from other batteries have all been recalled and are doing duty in the Co., the rest of the Co. were guard for Genl. Tyler (high position for a battalion of

Mass. 14th H. A.!) I can assure you it cut the Major badly; he was down on us probably for the game Col. Green played on him. He was drunk one quarter of the time, and when he is in that condition he comes down on the men hard, ties them to wheels and trees, fences, or any thing he can come across; it is shameful for a Genl. Comdg. over 200 pieces to do so. Genl. Meade gave him a jawing one day before the whole of us, for cutting up Genl. Kilpatrick's train; it was the second offence and when we left, heard that he was under arrest. We also saw Genl. Pleasanton with Genl. Meade. The men in the co. are glad to see men drafted at home; but wish $300 would not clear them; but then this is a rich man's war; the poor man has to do the fighting. We have been kicked about so long that no one knows what we are.

Lieut. Hervy has gone to Washington to try and get us back to the regiment. I hope he will succeed, most of the men want to go back, officers of course want to. The papers have just come, the news is what you might call "Bully." The cloud has passed over and things are looking more favorable. I for one would like to see this closed before winter. It greatly depends on Genl. Meade's abilities. As we stand a chance of going to Washington, you better direct there. We have travelled in all between 150 and 175 miles; good for new beginners?

Much love to all. Hoping this will find you well and enjoying things as they come, I remain,

Yours truly, L. Bradley, Jr.

MD. HEIGHTS, AUG. 2, 1863.

Dear Family:

Yours of July 20th and 27th arrived, the first we have had for a great while. We are enjoying the comforts of the old place on the Heights. At first it seemed lonesome, after travelling about as we had; another thing, the place was full of filth, the two regts. our Co. relieved, were the filthiest set of men I ever saw, that is if the neatness of their camp would be a proper thing to judge by. They tore bunks in barracks and built huts out doors. We are now alone by our selves, shall get things to looking as they did before, if work will do it. We did not go to Washington, neither did I want to go, Major R. was appointed for this post. He went to Washington to fill an order for guns and ammunition; while there he saw Genl. Halleck, he said that he had decided to keep this Batt. here, so we took our old places. We have now four 24 pdrs. Brass HOWtZ. and two 30 prd. parrotts. Killed a man yesterday, getting up one of the latter; he belonged in Co. H. John B. is dead, he died while in N. Y.; he was one of the men detailed in the 5th U. S. Art'y. Geo. Brick et is in the same Battery, we expect them back every day. There will be no need of your getting a map, we shall probably stop here the rest of our enlistment, unless we are put ofl". (It is well enough to put in.) I wish you could have seen this battalion when it first got back, rather a rough looking set; after eating so much salt pork and the hot days with it, a fellow would sweat well; when I wiped my face it was covered with nothing but pork and grease. Of course I looked clean when we came to a halt for the night! but then it did not hinder our sleeping. How different the affairs of the country look now from what they did a month ago. Lee defeated in Penn., Pemberton at Vicksburg, Gardner at Port Hudson and Bragg in Miss. I can assure you it has wrought a new feeling in the men; before all was defeat, but now it is victory. It pleases the men to see some of the men who were drafted; you may talk about its being a disgrace to be drafted, I say good enough for them; they would make a great fuss if Uncle Sam did not protect them and noAv they haven't got courage to help him. These men of course cannot think much of their country. Captain, you are not forgotten yet; many times a day, you are spoken of. This is what D. W. got off where Capt. H. heard him. "Pity we haven't got one of Bradley's old coats, in place of our commander now." On evacuating this place, I lost everything, now I want you to get up something and send to me. I thought for shirts you might get some cotton ones, such as you used to make when I was small, chequered ones, cut like a wool shirt. I think they would do best over the old flannel ones I am now picking up; but if you think best to get flannel ones, do so. Be sure and get flaps long enough. Another thing, I want stockings; the boots you sent last fall I have on now, but the tramp has played them out, got about ten holes in each. Do you think best to get a new pair now, or wait till Nov. I or won't it pay at allCan get them here for $6, but poor ones. Shoes $3.50. I must have something to my feet soon, so write in next what you think best to do. I will see what Jerry wants and let you know. Don't fail to make some kind of an answer, so I shall know what to do. Army clothing of the above named articles are very poor and high. Shirts $1.46 and are good for nothing. Much love to all.

Your Lev.

MD. HEIGHTS, AUG. 9, 1863.

Dear Family:

The old place really looks natural now we got it cleaned up. The men in the company are having a general run of sickness, a great many have been sick since we came back. Jere has been a little unwell for the past day or so and I myself feel a little indisposed. Since we came back I have had all the writing that I could possibly do, besides taking hold and fixing up the bunk and barrack. A great many of the guns on the mountain are being changed, the men have had to work very hard changing them. It took them one night and two days to get the 100 pdr. up. Charleston S. C. seems to draw the attention of all, no doubt we shall get it in time. I like the way Genl. Gilmore and Admiral Dalgreen go at the work. They seem to be determined to get the place and have all the honor to themselves. The army of the Potomac has got back very near its old camping ground. We have all sorts of rumors about moving. I believe none, till we get orders. I think I should like to go S. C. for the sake of seeing the country, but there is no possibility of our going. Captain, do you ever think of coming out here again . This is a pretty place and the scenery fine. The whole of you could come out; it would repay you for your trouble and expense. They are giving ten days furloughs now, any one can get them; but it hardly pays, only ten days! They are getting up a 2nd. H. A. regt. in Mass. are they not? I understand Lt. Hoppin has got a 1st Lieut, position in it. I presume, no chance for any one else. I might have had a strap by this time!

Hoping all are well, I remain Your Lev.

MD. HEIGHTS, SEPT. 6, 1863.

Dear Family:

Yours rec'd and contents noted. Glad to hear of your good health. Lieut. F. said you were looking well. Rec'd shirts by corp'l Frye. I wore them three days and was obliged to take them off or pass for a black man. The black came oft in profusion. It took nearly half a day to wash it off my body. I would really like to hear that piano. I presume it would sound very unnatural, as I never heard one in the old house, and I believe I have not heard one since I have been out here. I often think does the poor old pear tree bear well this year 'i I used to think it was the nicest fruit on the farm.

I got a pass Friday, for the purpose of obtaining all the information I could in regard to growing tobacco, as that was your desire. After about an hours work in getting through the chopped down trees (to stop the Rebs) I at length reached the valley. I asked one of the assistants about it and he referred me to an old negro, who had grown tons of it in his day; but by his looks, should think he had done about all the work he could do. And now, if the reader will give me his entire attention for a few moments I will explain all. (How does that sound?) A side hill or slope where the sun shines most of the day is preferable, new ground is the best; burn bush over the ground, in order to kill the weeds; then grub up the ground, working in ashes, "the more the better;" rake the ground up fine and then sow the tobacco, raking it w'ell. After raking and cross raking and rolling (as you do most of your land), I suppose that the tobacco would grow well. It neither needs wet not dry soil, but about the common soil. It greatly depends on the season, about the last of march is the time for planting in this section; it is sown the same as grass seed, only not so thick. It is not necessary to use manure.

The heavens are assuming a dark and cloudy aspect, and the low thunder rumbling in the distance, from the Allegany's, gives tokens of a refreshing shower. It is a beautiful sight to see from this point the wind and rain come rushing down the valley, seeming to the looker on as if he were above them all. Since we have been here I have seen a thunder shower below me in the valley.

Hoping this will find you all well, I remain &c. Lev.

MD. HEIGHTS, SEPT. 25, 1863.

Dear Mother:

Please find enclosed $100 and forward $45 to Uncle F. from Geo., being four month's pay. Credit me with $35 and Jerry $20. Practiced with our battery yesterday; fired 12 shots from 30 pdr Parrott. Range was over 3½ miles. They are splendid pieces. Co. H fired the 100 pdr last week; fired 5 miles, went through a small hill ricochet from there about 3 miles. I look to Rosecrans' army for great successes.

I remain. Very respectfully yours

L. Bradley, Jr.

Co. B 14th Mass. (H. A.)

MD. HEIGHTS, OCT. 4, 1963.

Mrs. Leverett Bradley,

Bradley Farm, Methuen, Mass.

Dear Family:

Rec'd yours. Contents noted. Glad to hear you are well, hope this will find you in good condition; yours found us well.

Only think, nine (9) more months only and our time will be out; every day is counted and deducted from the original. After my time is out here I intend to enlist in the Home Guards. I forgot the letter yesterday and hope you will not be worried because it does not reach sooner. Have you ever heard of the two corps of the army of the Potomac going to reinforce Rosecrans? They went by this rout. How would you treat a fellow if he should get home about Thanksgiving time? Well, I suppose. Yesterday was occupied in getting the men to sign the clothing rolls and books. Got through with it first rate. Last night was terribly cold, slept about four hours and during that time was in a double bow knot. Went to a dance at Sandy Hook the other night, had a fine time; the girls are very agreeable although they are Marylanders.

Much love to all. I remain,
L. Bradley, Jr.
Co. B 1st Mass. H. A.

P. S. Will try and write more next time. The box has not come.

HOWTZ. BATTERY, MD. HEIGHTS, OCT. 18, 1863.

Dear Friends:

Yours rec'd. Today has been an exciting one to us, there has been a big engagement ten miles from here; we have driven the rebs nearly ten miles towards Berryville, have been at it all day, and now I can hear the roar of the artillery; we are making every thing to resist the rebels. We may have a chance to show the " Johnnies" what we are made of. At last accounts, Meade was slowly working this way, covering Washington during the march; should not be surprised to see the Army of the Potomac at any time. In the late movements of the Army of the Potomac considerable strategy was used; so far, we have got the best of it. I have no doubt Lee contemplates making another raid into Md. and Penn. I think the movement the rebels are making here now is to destroy the Baltimore and Ohio R. R. We have got a new Genl. now, his name is Sullivan, formerly with Genl. Grant as inspector Genl.; marched in to Vicksburg July 4th; he is a fine looking man and a son in law of Genl Kelly, who commanded here before the evacuation. There has been a lull in the battle for some time; but now the ball has opened again in good earnest. But they are working from us fast. We saved Frank's phiz during the other march and shall try to, if we have to march again. The men have all gone out to work on the battery. This will probably stop all furloughs, so shall not get mine.

MONDAY.

Nothing new. Some say it is the advance of Lee's army, others that the guerillas, combined, are trying to call us out and let Lee in.

LEV.

HOWTZ. BATTERY, MD. HEIGHTS, NOV. 15, 1863.

Dear Family:

Yours found us well and enjoying ourselves to the best advantage. Yesterday the wind was very boisterous and strong, beating the water through the mud on the barracks and wetting things inside.

We have just started a barrack or dance hall, forty feet long by fourteen wide; are anticipating great times as soon as we get it finished. It is a big project as boards are very scarce, expect to have to send to Williamsport Md. for them; it is a company concern and have got nearly $75 subscribed already.

George, I should like to go to the singing school with you; don't know as it would be very good, but then of course any one expects a little fun at such places. Re-enlistment papers are expected every day. If matters go on as they have for the last month or so, I think it is a poor inducement to enlist. News is not very brilliant; but from what we can hear, there is a general forward movement the whole line. The way things are now, a man would not like to be taken prisoner; they are trying their best to starve them, and so far have been very successful. The evenings are beginning to be quite long and we pass them off very agreeably by getting a negro in and getting him to dancing; he is sure to go as long as the music lasts, we have a great deal of sport with them.

Much love to all.

HOWTZ. BATTERY, MD. HEIGHTS, NOV. 21, 1863.

Dear Family:

I am in receipt of yours. Glad to hear of your continued good health. It has been raining all day, so the boys for enjoyment all flock to our barrack, where they have dancing and music &c.. and by great exertion have passed so much of the day off. I improve this opportunity to answer my weekly epistle. You seem to feel a great deal of anxiety about our, or I might say, my re-enlisting. Now you don't want that little (now ordinary sized fellow at home, that used to, in days gone by, do all the mischief and gener-ally get all the blame for it! That is all I will say, but wait and see what kind of an answer I get. But to relieve your minds on this important point, I will say, so far, not a man of Co. B has re-enlisted, and the reason is, no one has been here to re-enlist them. And as for the future, you need not worry at all about either of us. In one sense of the word, every man ought to re-enlist; the country is in great need of men. A man that has any patriotism in him ought to do it and money shall be no object. But as for me, I feel that I have risked myself through one three years, and I will wait until every able bodied man does the same before trying it again. Sometimes I feel sad to think that I could not visit home this coming Thanksgiving, and then again I think there was no need (sickness) of going and I am glad I did not go. The fact is we are enjoying ourselves now very well and time passes so rapidly, it seems as if it were but a little while longer to stop. I shall endeavor to enjoy myself here but hope you will there. We have signed the pay rolls and have been expecting, for two days past. I shall have to close here, so as to get things ready for the pay-master to pay more rapidly, as it is raining outside.

Monday, 23rd.

We were paid off Sat.; all went off smoothly. The furloughed men started for home at 2 o'clk. this morning, just the right time! I think they ought to enjoy themselves and probably will. The box if it has not been sent need not come till Christmas. They cost too much to send often. George says he expects his father (uncle Frank) out here this week; will wait and send my money by him, which will save a little.

Lev.

Fort Whipple, Va., Dec. 18, 1863.

Dear Father:

Yours of Sunday last was rec'd in due time. Also started off directly to dun; saw Capt. Andrew; he said that there was about $130.00 that he had not collected from the mess, but would wait until next pay day and see if he could get it, and if not take it from his own pocket. As for Capt. Hosmer, I know where he is, being at Washington with the position of Asst. Judge Advocate Genl. Now I can hardly summon the pluck to dun him, being in that position, so I think it would be better to wait until some further day and if any opportunity offers I will improve it.

We are beginning to get acquainted with fancy soldiering now; all have to come out in gloves, being furnished the first time and having to supply yourself the next. It makes a great difference with the looks of the men. Uncle Frank Bricket called over today. I asked him what the prospect was of our ever owning Bradley Farm; he told me (as no doubt he has told you before). It really seems to me that something ought to be done. There has been money spent on the place, if that is all it wants, but it seems to me we are no nearer the end we are after. Uncle Frank spoke of a farm up in Hampstead. How did you like it;

presume you would not like to swap. We are very much attached to the old place, all of us; but that should not hinder us from leaving it if we can do better some where else and especially when in the condition we are. I should consider that a very cheap price for a farm (I mean the one he showed you) if as good as he says it is. I do almost feel that the old farm will never amount to any thing. It wants making all over new and th9.t is a very hard task. I should think you would be discouraged after spending nearly all your years so far on it and not coming out better; but it shows the Bradleys never have that failing. How much is the debt now and what interest do you have to pay. I suppose it takes all you have to pay the interest? How does George feel about leaving it and the rest of them. Don't want to, I 'll bet! Write all particulars and let me know about it for once; you know you never were much for telling your business matters to the rest of the family, and besides it is right I should know. They all say that I am my own master now, but I do not ask that privilege yet, whether or no I have a right to claim it. So far 20 have re-enlisted and I guess that is all that will. Shall send $20 home by uncle Frank, part or nearly all of which is Jerry's. Things are awfully high at the present time. Love to all. I remain

L. Bradley, Jr.
Co. B. 1st Mass. H. Arty.

To L. Bradley, Esq.

[His claim as a veteran made him and others consider him "of age." Ed.]

Fort Whipple, Va., Dec. 4, 1868.

Dear Father:

Yours of Sunday last was perused with great care and contents noted. You wanted to know my mind about matters ! I should make a very poor judge, as I do not know how things look now. But I should say stick to it, if there is any chance at all, because we have put already work enough into it to make three farms. I know nothing out this way for you to do. About being discharged; when the regiment is to be has not been decided yet: some of the recruits have written Gov. Andrew and he says that they " will be discharged with the rest," so I take it for granted we shall be. As to the matter of a choice of regiments when re-enlisting 't If I understand it right, a man can choose, provided the Reg't he is in is not kept up, and the Reg't he chooses is not full; but it must be a Reg't from the state he belongs to.

He must also keep in the old Reg't until its three years are up and then they have the choice. Write me what your intentions are of doing, as soon as warm weather comes. Do you have rheumatism to trouble you again t Last night I slept terribly cold. The barracks are not as good as a barn, boards only one inch thick and layed on like clapboards; besides the barracks are on piles about four feet long, so as to give a clean sweep underneath.

They are very strict about the barracks, will allow no shelves or anything of that kind. The bunks are all moveable. In fact everything has a place here. Shall begin on muster rolls tomorrow. Yours &c.

Lev.

FORT WHIPPLE, VA., JAN. 10, 1864.

Dear Friends:

Yours of last Sabbath duly rec'd found us well. We have been having very cold weather, but Jerry and I have got straw now and sleep very comfortably, and as that is one of the most essential duties of a soldier, and among them all the one he likes best, I guess that we shall, if divine providence favors us, this winter. Have been trying every opportunity to get over to Corbets but as yet have not succeeded; he lives the other side of the line of rifle pits, and in order to visit him I shall have to obtain a pass from Brigade Head Quarters. Will certainly seize the first opportunity. It is not very comfortable writing this, they are beating " tattoo" right under the window, and they are soul stirring strains; but then I don't fancy them. I expect Jerry has written a long letter and as I get enough of that business just this time of the year, you will please excuse this abrupt leaving off. We only have an hour between "tattoo" and "taps." Much love to all. Good-night.

From Lev.

Diary and Memoranda, 1864

Fort Whipple, Jan. 7, 1864,.

This little book was obtained by the earnest wish of my Mother, who desired I should keep a record of events that transpire, during the new year we have just entered.

Lev.

Jan. 1st A new year has commenced and before its close I hope peace may be restored to our country. And all be restored to their peaceful homes.

Jan. 3rd Attended divine service in the bomb proof this afternoon. Sermon discourse from James 4th, 14th verse. Had singing by the audience, and music from the band (America).

Jan. 7th No new army movements. Reports say they have gone into winter quarters. Two months ago the "Astor House" dissolved itself! passed the day reading "Under the Spell."

Jan. 8th The Potomac has frozen over, consequently un-navigable. Today is the anniversary of the battle of New Orleans. The Co rec'd 22 recruits, none that I knew. Steamers passed down the river today; but it was hard work.

Jan. 11th No news of importance. There was a grand dinner given at the Fort by Genl. Barnard to his friends. If I could judge by their faces, should say they had a good time. I issued clothing today, and got through it very well.

Jan. 12th Major Cole whipped the guerilla Mosely in the Shenandoah valley. Have worked all day copying orders. Saw a palmetto leaf for the first time.

Jan. 13th Gillmore is still knocking at the gates of Charleston. Jere went to the city today. The first lot of Vet. Vol. on furlough have returned today; most all have seen father and say he is looking well.

Jan. 16th Were inspected by Major R. today. Any amount of growling, mud knee deep. Expect to be inspected again tomorrow. Vets are beginning to resign to their fate. Some thoughts of re-enlisting.

Jan. 17th Copied barrack rules. There are skaters on the river.

Jan. 20th Rec'd a lot of letters; getting to have lots of correspondents, must appreciate my letters. Of course I do my best; hut 1 think they are dry. Lieut C. has any amount, he is a fine fellow.

Jan. 21st Several of the non-commissioned officers have asked to be reduced to the ranks, Col. T. is issuing orders by the bushel, very unpopular at the present time. Have got to come out on parade in the future.

Jan. 22nd Quite a hubbub kicked up in the Co. amongst the non coms.; five are now in the guard house and one in arrest, grand chance for promotion. I have been making out charges and specifications all the evening against the non-coms. They will be tried by a genl. court martial.

Jan. 23rd Drew rations today. G—n is in the guard house. I have just returned from the Arlington House; heard some guitar playing that was enough to put me above the clouds.

Jan. 24th Beautiful evening. Makes one think of home when he goes out to take a walk.

Jan. 25th All the non-coms returned to duty today. I am at work on "Clothing book," copying from old book to a new one.

Jan. 26th A beautiful evening, the moon is shining brightly and the Potomac is all aglow. The capitol of our nation looks magnificent in its rays, and to cap it all, the Goddess of Liberty smiles on the scene (poetic!)

Jan. 28th Have been preparing all day for inspection which comes off tomorrow. Played four games of chess for the first time.

Jan. 29th Inspection passed off well on the part of the men; but the officers lacked a little knowledge in the infantry drill.

Jan. 30th Had a parade this eveg. in a heavy mist; the guns are looking too well to keep dry I

Jan. 31st A very unpleasant day. Of course did not prevent inspection and parade. Have been writing ever since supper time on Monthly returns, furloughs, &c.

Feb. 1st Quite a change in the Brigade Staff. Col. T. has sent them all to their companies, having found that they were working a plot. Some think in the end that the officers will get the best of it.

Feb. 3rd. Went to the Washington theatre last night. Miss Keene played "She stoops to conquer." It was a laughable affair. She did look splendidly arrayed in all her beauty, before the foot lights, a splendid form; but paint was too profuse, I would rather have seen her natural complexion.

Feb. 12th A rumor has been circulated that we are going to Texas. I hope it is true, as I have a great desire to see that part of the country.

Feb. 13th Had a close inspection by Col. T. Did not give any companies much praise. Carried a knapsack all the time, a very pretty and useful article for a soldier.

Feb. 14th Took a walk today and visited Forts Craig and Albany, also hospital and saw Geo. Frye [cousin]; he has had a rough time of it.

Feb. 15th Our going to Texas is played out, the 2nd. Conn, is going. Got a pipe tonight drawn by a lottery ticket.

Feb. 22nd A rumor, viz. Genl. Sherman has taken 1200 prisoners and is now marching on Mobile.

Feb. 23rd The pay master visited us and gave us our XXVI. for two months hard labor. The officers had a big time at Lt. Col. W's place last night; some of them (I should judge by their manners) had touched the cup.

Feb. 24th Had a horse back ride in the morning. In the evening, went to Grover's theatre [Washington, D. C.]. Edwin Booth took the part of Ruy Blas. The house cheered him several times, it was the first time that I ever saw him. I liked him very much, he made a slave of me. I would speak of the female portion; but they had such large mouths there is not room here to put them in. No reliable news from Genl. Sherman; but he is still on the move. Longstreet is retreating from the front of Knoxville. Went to the theatre. The play was Brutus. I liked it much; it made some of the women cry. He makes me his captive. March 3rd. Have felt a little indisposed all day; but before dark summoned courage to visit the Grovers' theatre. The play was "Othello." I did not get very interested in the piece, doubtless on account of Booth not taking the part of Othello. It was sustained by all the actors.

Mar. 5th Heard from Genl. Kilpatrick, who has been making a raid on Richmond; it is acknowledged a bold affair by the southern press. Absent from inspection; rec'd my deserts for it.

Mar. 12th Camp life begins to look like a dull affair; am not so anxious to come out with my pretty gun as at first. Have just come in from parade, have eaten supper and now my thoughts wander to friends and relatives at home and the good times I used to have. It would be impossible to count the number of times that my mind turns toward it during the day, still I am contented.

Mar. 21st On account of slight illness I have been unable to keep my book. On the 16th, Co. B moved to Fort Woodbury. I like it very well. Col. T. is trying to get the Reg't into the field as Light Infantry; I hope he will succeed. I intend to re-enlist tomorrow.

Mar. 25th I am a Veteran Volunteer and of course stuck for three years more! Going over after bounty and pay tomorrow. Do not intend to take my furlough till May. Three years more seems a long time but guess I am good for it.

Mar. 31st It is just a week ago that I took the oath to stand by the flag three years more. Have had quite a correspondence from home; I guess they are not dissatisfied.

Apr. 5th Went to the theatre on Monday, where Edwin Forrest was playing Macbeth. It was the first time I ever saw him. It was splendid. I must say there is a charm in tragedy that captivates me.

May 7th Arriv'd home on vet. furlough.

May 19th (At home) The 1st Mass. H. A. in action. Co. B lost more than any company in the Regiment [53 killed and wounded]. George Bricket was killed.

[Up to this time, besides his duty as private in the ranks, he had also been serving as company clerk. lie was at home on a veteran's furlough in May, 1864, when the regiment was ordered to join the advance of the whole army under Grant, and he was obliged to read in the papers of the terrible loss it sustained in the battle of the Wilderness on May 19th, where, in the afternoon, while repulsing Ewell's corps, the regiment lost in one short hour 898 men. His own Company, B, lost in killed and wounded over half of their entire number. In this battle his cousin George Wellington Brickett, of Company B, was instantly killed in the first charge made on the enemy, and another cousin, Asa Frye, was wounded. Fortunately, his brother, also a member of the company, but acting at the time as regimental bugler, escaped uninjured. With these terrible facts before him, it required a great deal of courage to leave home to join the regiment, knowing that a severe campaign was before them. He rejoined the regiment during the last day of the battle of Cold Harbor, and was first under fire with the regiment, fighting as infantry, at the first assault on Petersburg by the Second Army Corps, to which the regiment was attached,

on the evening of June 16. when the regiment again lost heavily. Leverett received a bullet through his shirt-sleeve which lodged in his coat, which was rolled on his back. The coat had some eight different holes in it, and was a wonderment to all those who saw it the next day, when it was exhibited. Ed.]

June 3rd Started for the scene of war. Father went with me to Boston. (He was ordered to go by Albany on business by the Capt. of his company.)

June 4th Arrived in X. Y.

June 5th Arrived in Washington.

June 6th Went over to Fort Albany and found some of the boys.

June 7th Started for Washington to go to the Army of the Potomac; was too late.

June 8th Started for the "White House Landing," Va., on steamer Lizzie Baker. Had a splendid sail.

June 9th Arrived at White House and started for the Army: went ten miles and stopped for the night.

June 10th Arrived at Gaines Mills and found the boys. They looked rough. Only fifty present. Pickets firing all day.

June 11th Pickets firing all day.

June 12th Saw John W. breathe his last. Started at 10 p.m. on a flank movement; marched about 8 miles and halted for the night.

June 13th Started bright and early; crossed the Chickahominy at noon and halted for the night, about two miles from the James river. I was detailed for picket, but was relieved; commenced to put up breast works. Marched during the day 25 miles and was very tired.

June 14th Started at 10 a.m. for James river; embarked on a steamer and landed the other side; marched two miles and halted for the rest of the column; formed line of battle and stopped for the night.

June 15th Set out at 10 a.m. on the Petersburg pike; had gone ten miles when we heard firing; got to the extreme front at 12 M. The negro troops had taken four lines of the enemy's works.

June 16th *[First Assault on Petersburg.]* About six a.m. the enemies Artillery opened on us, our batteries were soon in position, and silenced their fire. Built breast works and at six p.m. the whole line moved forward on a charge, we were soon hotly engaged, we gained about half a mile of ground. Co. B had 8 wounded. I was struck by two spent balls.

June 17th Moved forward half a mile on the right of the road, layed all night, the Artillery threw shells over us, at night, which was not very pleasant. Did not have a good night's rest.

[Mr. Bradley's brother. Col. J. Payson Bradley, sends me his account of Leverett's first battle. Ed.]

INCIDENT IN THE ASSAULT ON PETERSBURG, JUNE 16, 1864

On our march to Petersburg on the afternoon of June 16th we could hear the heavy firing caused by Smith's Division of the Army of the James in its attack on the outer works. We reached Petersburg after dusk, and laid on our arms all night.

Early on the morning of June 16, being in line of battle, we were opened on by a confederate battery which was soon silenced by the effective fire of a battery of the Fifth United States Artillery. Just before sunset we were given intrenching-tools and the whole division advanced into the woods, with instructions to gain a certain position and throw up earthworks. We had not advanced more than a hundred yards when we were met by a terrific fire of musketry from the enemy directly in our front. Intrenching tools were dropped and the fire was returned, and then began a battle royal which lasted until ten o'clock in the evening. The enemy were determined to drive us from the woods, and we were as determined to hold our position, which we did until morning, when by a flank movement the enemy were obliged to fall back.

This was Leverett's first battle with the regiment when fighting as infantry. I remember he went into the fight in his shirt-sleeves and was the only man that I saw in the regiment who had on a white shirt, which of course made him a conspicuous mark. You see he had but lately returned from his veteran furlough and had not had time in which to draw a woolen shirt from the quartermaster. He did not show the least fear, and, in fact, during all our campaigning, I never saw him hesitate for a moment to take his proper position, whether in the ranks or as a non-commissioned officer, and by his example inspire the men around him.

I very well remember the stubbornness of this battle of June 16th. Acting at the time as the colonel's orderly as well as regimental bugler, I was directed to the ordnance officer with instructions to send up extra ammunition, and I think that three times during the afternoon and evening the cartridge-boxes of the men were filled from the ammunition supply-wagons.

I lost sight of Leverett soon after the engagement began, and of course was very anxious as to his safety; but it was not until after the firing ceased, between ten and eleven o'clock at night, and our regiment had been relieved from the first line of battle and was taking up its position a little to the rear, that I recognized the white flag of Massachusetts, which, although it was of course after sunset, had never been furled. It was being carried in the hands of one of the color corporals, as the color sergeant, who carried it into the fight, had just passed away from a fearful wound received about eight o'clock in the evening. (Not until, however, I had had the satisfaction of giving him a refreshing draught of water from the canteen I was carrying.)

It was a bright moonlight night, and no one can describe the feeling that was in my heart as I scanned the thin ranks of the regiment as they moved to the rear, looking for the one man above all others who was so dear to me, my brother Leverett. I soon made out the white shirt-sleeves. Although surrounded by the men of his company, I broke through the ranks and in a minute more we were in each other's arms, hugging and kissing each other like a couple of sentimental schoolgirls, and our first inquiry to each other was, "Are you wounded.'" Then he showed me the two bullet-holes through his shirt-sleeves and the mark on his arm where the missile had just grazed him. This is the bullet that went into the coat rolled on his back, making eight separate holes in it.

I made the remark, "You must have killed every Johnny Reb in front of you, for I have been sending up ammunition to the line of battle all the afternoon from the ordnance train." (I was told by some of the men earlier in the evening that they had fired as high as eighty rounds apiece.) He coolly replied, "No, let 's see;" and on looking at his cartridge-box said, "I have only fired eleven rounds." I said, "How 's that, Leverett.'" and he replied, "Why, I only fired when I saw something io fire at." I asked him what he thought of the battle, and how he liked soldiering as an infantryman, and he replied, " It was rather hot at times, and at the end I was so completely exhausted and so choked from the fumes of sulphur that I fell asleep just where I was lying, behind some temporized earthworks, although at the time a battery of twelve-pounder Napoleon guns were firing over our heads at the enemies' earthworks on the crest of the hill in our front."

June 18th *[Second assault on Petersburg.]* Started on a charge about 5 A.M. Got one line of th^ir breast-works. Moved forward to about 500 yds. of their next and threw up rifle-pits. In the afternoon a charge was ordered; but "no go."

June 19th We were relieved from this position and placed in a worse place ! We threw up rifle pits to support a battery. Worked all night; moved forward and commenced to throw more works.

June 20th Layed in the same position all day. The sharpshooters were firing. It was a sight to see the dead on the field, where the 1st. Maine charged. Moved to the rear and left about 12 o'clock.

June 21st Started on the road about 9 a.m. to cut the Weldon and Richmond Railroad. Arrived about noon; moved towards the Rebs and fortified. Remained all night.

June 22nd Moved forward about ^ a mile and erected riflepits. A Reb. battery annoyed us considerably. About noon, firing was heard directly in front. Soon after Barlow's Div. came rushing over our rifle-pits, the Rebs followed. Engaged them a short time and fell back. Loss: Co. B 8 wounded.

June 23rd Our brigade was moved to the left to support a battery. Shortly after an artillery duel began. The shell all went over the battery and came amongst us. We lost one man wounded. Just at dusk a charge was ordered to be made by our division across an open field. We drove the Rebs back and threw up rifle-pits. Remained in rifle-pits all day; buried our dead; were relieved at night and went to the rear.

THE DEW DROP RESTAURANT

493 Tenth Street

Near Pennsylvania Avenue

CHOICE WINES, LIQUORS, AND CIGARS

[Written in pencil on the back of the above card.]

JUNE 23, 1864

We had a battle yesterday. I have not seen Jerry but he is in the rear somewhere. Do not entertain any fear about him, for he can take care of himself. Co. B had 22 men at roll call last night; some more will probably come in C.— W.—. F.—, and R.—. are wounded.

Lev.

Get me a chance somewhere if you can. Have heard from Jerry, he is all right. George Frye is missing. I think is prisoner. Capt. K. is killed. Love to all. Will write every opportunity. We got the worst of it yesterday'. Lev.

[This was in front of Petersburg, Va. Ed.]

In Camp Near Petersburg, Va., July 3, 1864.

Dear Family:

We rec'd a letter on the 1st. inst. which found us all well. Jerry has been ordered back to Head Quarters, to blow the calls for the Regt. Since I wrote last we have moved forward about a mile and built very strong rifle-pits. The whole army (as much as we know about it) is at a stand still. It would be impossible this hot weather to move; rumors say, we are waiting for re-enforcements, which we need badly enough.

I must say I found things a great deal different from what I expected; any one is lucky, who gets out of a fight. And even those who get a flesh wound are lucky. Some, in the army even, shoot off a finger to get rid of going into action; the latter are not thought much of. Flesh wounds are worth from ten to twenty dollars. But during this hot weather slight flesh wounds have proved fatal. This is considered by old soldiers the hardest campaign of the war so far; until the last few days, some part of the line has been engaged. The genl. health of the troops is good; but I would not believe before I came out here that man was capable of enduring so much. Today, half the army would be sick in bed if they were at home, but here they go well with the well ones. Nothing is so tiresome work as fighting. During the action of the 16th., which I wrote you about, our line of battle got separated: and some of us went to the left and the regt. to the right. We were ordered over to the Regt. but we formed a line about half way. There were no Rebs in our immediate front at the time, but the right was hotly engaged; we layed down and I got a short nap before we were relieved. The Artillery in the rear throwing shell over our heads all the time. I used to hear them speak of the first Bull Run, but hardly credited the story till I experienced it myself. We were relieved the other day quite suddenly, by Genl. Ewells and Hill's corps; not a very welcome relief. It is almost impossible to get water, consequently, the boys are very dirty and as a natural consequence we have plenty of those little, called in natural history "lice." Some of the boys have come better flank movements on them than Grant did on the Rrebs at North Anna, by turning all their clothing wrong side out; it takes about two days for them to crawl onto the other side, then change them again; they soon get disgusted and leave. I have been hard at work for the last few days with back papers, muster, and muster-out rolls. The July boys are anxious to get off. The general opinion is that the Co.s will be consolidated. Officers are in an awful fix about who is going home; they all want to go. I hardly think you enjoyed my furlough much more than I did; at least, I should not complain if they would give me another. George Frye [a cousin] has been heard from; he is in prison without doubt. Tell the folks not to worry about him; as there were a lot of them taken, will probably be sent to Georgia.

Give my regards to all enquiring friends. Much love to all.

Respectfully &c. L. Bradley, Jr.

Co. B 1st Mass. H. A. 2nd Brigade,

Army of the Potomac.

[A letter from their mother to Jerry.]

METHUEN, JULY 7, 1864.

My dear son Jed:

We received your kind letter of the 23rd in due time. I have not learned from either of you since; our anxiety is intense. We know you would write if possible, for the reason you always have. It may be the mail or something of that kind. Do write on receiving this, if you are alive.

I suppose those that are to come home from your company are on the road; how glad I should be if both of your times had been out; but I must wait with submission. I am dreading the sickly season. Do be as careful of yourself as possible, and let us know if you are sick.

Is it the same doctor you had at Harper's Ferry. Does the chaplain remain with you.

Grandmother's family are feeling bad about George. I hope he will keep well and have enough to eat. Does anybody know where they went, what part of the South? He may find his mother; she is in Mobile. His brother Milburn is not in the army, but at school, and so is Sarah.

We all feel anxious about you both; all we can do is to pray for you. Everybody enquires for you. Great praise is awarded Lev. for his courage and patriotism in leaving home at such a time. Everybody felt for him, but nobody can feel as I do. Such an anxiety no one but a mother feels.

I have written a few lines to your doctor. I felt as though I must. I shall enclose with this much love to Lev., and may God spare you both from sickness and death is the constant prayer of your mother.

Father is very busy commencing haying. Help is very scarce.

We are all well in body, but anxious in mind.

Mother.

July 4th It was the stillest fourth I ever passed; the boys had no chance to celebrate. Bands played in the evng. There was a little Artillery firing on the right; we expected an attack.

July 5th Worked on the company's papers. Boys are anxious to be off; but no prospect.

July 6th Were relieved at ten a.m.; marched half a mile to the rear, pitched camp, and went in earnest to get the men off. *[Time had expired.]*

July 7th Same old place. Something new comes up every minute. The boys begin to think they will never get away.

July 8th A little firing; the shell did damage where they struck, but none came near our camp.

July 9th The boys started for home at dusk; it seemed sad to part with them. We moved at 10 a.m. to the left.

July 10th Layed in the same place till afternoon and were relieved; went back to our old position.

July 11th Layed in the same place over night and next day. Moved at 12 midnight to the left, encamped in a field. *[18th birthday.]*

July 12th Layed in the same place all day and all night; it. The sun visited and spent the day with us. Sand knee deep.

July 13th Moved 2½ miles to the right, at 7 A.M. Had to pick our way, the dust so thick could not see far ahead. Had the sun as usual.

July 17th Layed in this place all day. At night we moved front and went to tearing down Rebel rifle-pits. Moved back in the morning.

July 22nd Layed in the same place for a week. Moved to the left today about a mile. Are now protecting the flank of the army.

July 26th Started at 6 p.m.; marched towards City Point, turned off and crossed the Appomattox and James. Rested but twice the whole march, about 20 miles; the corps straggled very badly.

July 27th *[Battle of Strawberry Plains.]* Skirmishing began almost as soon as we got to the north side of the James. Captured 4 guns. Johnnies were surprised to find that we had got out to intercept them.

July 28th Layed in the woods all day. Saw some of the 26th regt. At 9 o'clock P.M. we started for the front of Petersburg; marched till morning, about 20 miles.

July 29th Layed in the woods all day (the 3rd div.), at night relieved; some of the 18th corps in the trenches. Rebs began shelling us. The siege of Petersburg has begun in earnest.

July 30th *[Explosion of the mine.]* A regular artillery battle began at 4 P.M. The shell flew thick; were relieved at 10 p.m., marched to our old camp. Burnside blew up a rebel fort, and 500 Rebs and 18 guns were buried.

July 31st Drew rations as soon as we arrived in camp. Layed in camp all day and night.

Aug. 1st Started back for our old camp in the woods at 9 a.m. I was detailed to report at Regt. Head Quarters.

Aug. 2nd Working at Head Qrs.

Aug. 7th Have been working on papers; in the same position. Almost starved to death, but fun if the boys have any grub on hand.

Aug. 12th Same position till today; started at 2 o'clk for City Point, arrived at 7 o'clk. It was terribly hot, a great many were sunstruck.

Aug. 13th Layed on a hill all day. At 5 p.m. embarked on steamer Octorora; ran down the river about 3 miles, when the whole expedition started up the river. In all, about 20 vessels.

Aug. 14th Disembarked at Deep Bottom. 1st and 2nd Divs. went into the woods and we layed in the sun. The 10th corps captured 6 guns. Layed here all night; rainy.

Aug. 15th *[Battle of Deep Bottom.]* Started at 9 a.m. for the right, having been assigned to the 19th corps of our Brigade; skirmish for four hours, through a dense forest to enable our cavalry to pass out on the right flank. Lost one killed and 7 wounded.

Aug. 16th Moved to the left in the morning, and to front at 10 a.m. Our regt. in reserve. 10th corps charged well and took 800 prisoners. We performed several duties during the day. There was hard fighting all day. We lost one man (was taken sick and went to the rear).

Aug. 17th Fell in with the Brigade as it passed on their way to our old Div. Layed in a close mass all day; it rained hard.

Aug. 18th Layed in the same place until dark, rained; started for the front of Petersburg, walked all night; rained a little. Marched until Morning of the 19th

Aug. 19th Kept on marching to the left, were put on picket. 9th and 5th Corps moved to the left. Have taken the Weldon R. R. Rebs came on to us, and took about 50 prisoners (on the run).

Aug. 20th Same place. I stopped at the regt. hospital.

Aug. 22th I returned to the regt.

Aug. 25th Were ordered to the left at 3 p.m. The Rebs began to shell us as we left; moved about five miles through up the works and came back.

Aug. 26th The regt. was detailed for picket. I sat up till 11.30 p.m. and was relieved.

Aug. 28th Worked on Muster rolls. Did not know that it was Sunday.

Aug. 29st Nothing of importance here. Geo. B. McClellan nominated Candidate for the Chicago Convention. Platform, purely "Peace on any terms."

Aug. 31st Finished up the Rolls and were mustered for six weeks pay by the Major.

Sept. 1st The regt. moved forward 400 yards and occupied a fort.

Sept. 4th At 12 o'clk our guns fired a salute on the capture of Atlanta. The Rebs replied with shell and we answered and for a while the shot fell thick.

Sept. 11th During this time we have been laying in the same camp, the Artillery firing on our right. It has gotten to be an old thing.

Sept. 24th Here I am sitting in my tent, where I have been at work all day; the rest of the boys have gone to bed. We have had glorious news from Sheridan, in the valley. Give salutes with shotted guns.

Sept. 25th Were relieved and went into camp in the rear,

Sept. 29th Lay as support, all the time ready to re-enforce any part of the Hue. Butler took 3000 prisoners and 15 guns.

Oct. 1st Took the cars at 1 p.m. for the left, a terrible storm was raging; layed in a mass all the afternoon.

Oct. 2nd Moved to left early and supported the skirmishing line. The records of the day I shall not chronicle, but I shall never forget them. Moved back at night for fear we should get flanked.

[It is told in the regiment's history what he declined to tell: " The brigade was ordered to make a demonstration on the enemy's works, to ascertain their strength and, if possible, carry them. As we advanced the enemy opened a battery that was masked in the angle of his works, having a raking fire with canister and spherical case. Our support not coming up, we were obliged to retire. It was a very .stubborn fight; officers and men were killed, wounded, and taken prisoners. It was known as "Poplar Grove fight." Ed.]

Oct. 6th Went in to our old camp at Fort Hayes.

Oct. 20th Moved about 11 p.m. to the rear and closed, en masse.

Oct. 25th. Waiting orders; cold nights.

Oct. 26th At two P.M. moved to the "yellow house."

Oct. 27th *[Battle of Boydton Plank Rd.]* Moved early, began skirmishing in forenoon; drove Rebs 4 miles and got a position at 4 o'clk. Got a severe shelling and had a small fight, retreating after dark; pickets gobbled, severe attack, loss of life fearful.

Oct. 28th Moved back to our old camp in the rear.

Oct. 30th Moved back to our old position *[Fort Alexander Hayes]* in the works.

Nov. 4th Went down to Div. Hospital; took Jerry's rifle. His furlough was a surprise.

[Jerry was very ill and Leverett and the colonel succeeded in getting him a furlough. It was made out giving him leave to go home to vote. He was bugler of the regiment and only sixteen years old ! He got through the journey as far as the train from New York to Boston. There he entered the car so weak he could hardly stand. The car was crowded; but he was made to feel how little the people of the North realized the hardship of the soldiers' lives, for they pushed by him as a vagabond and he sank exhausted on the floor in the corner of the car and could not keep back the tears. Ed.]

Nov. 8th Abraham Lincoln re-elected President of the United States of America by a large majority over Genl. Geo. B. McClellan, candidate of the Chicago Convention.

Jerry arrived home; met father and mother at the village.

FORT HAYES, NEAR PETERSBURG, VA., NOV. 14, 186.

Dear Family:

Yours of the 6th inst arrived in due time. I have been waiting anxiously to hear from Jere, as he promised to write as soon as he got home.

The process of getting mustered out should receive particular attention. I shall forward today his descriptive list, to Major Clark, Boston, Mass. I would advise Jerry to report without delay, after the receipt of this, and do the best he can, for his furlough and term of service expire at the same time.

The weather has been changeable for the past fortnight. At first it was exceedingly cold, then we began to have the beautiful Indian summer. The days weie perfectly delightful and the nights equally so; but now it seems as if cold winter had fairly set in. but we are fully prepared for him, with a large fire place and a comfortable sheebang. There have been quite a number of promotions in the regt.; doubtless you have read of them in the papers. There was a great deal of surprise expressed when the commissions came, for some have received them that we supposed stood no chance at all; two of them, B and A n. have been in only one fight (the first) and have played ever since. The quarter master Sergt. was promoted, Which left a vacancy there. I was asked for; but the Major refused to let me go, on the grounds that he wanted me here, to do the writing for the companies B and C. I think they are not using me exactly right; but still I shall not complain; but one thing is, he is discouraging good behavior and a soldierly bearing; but it shall not serve to move me from a straight and forward course. No one has gone as yet, and they know of no one to send. So perhaps I shall get it yet; but I shall not expect it. Promotions have been made in the Regiment by the Gov. without the sanction of the Regt. Commander. I am not particularly desirous of another lift, but if you think best and should some day have a chance to speak to some influential man, it would have a great weight in the matter. I understand now that names have been forwarded to the Gov. for promotion; but ignorant who they are Genl. Hancock has tried to get this Corps to the rear in camp, but was unsuccessful. I for one was glad of it.

Old Fort days seem like home. Love to all.

L. Bradley, Jr.

[He was made quartermaster-sergeant. Ed.]

HEAD QUARS. CO. B 1ST MASS. H. A., DEC. 4, 1864.

Dear Family:

Your last was rec'd in due time. Since I last wrote our whole Corps has moved, relieving the 19th at the left of the line. The duties in front of Petersburg were too hard for this corps, with too small numbers. We are now in a fine forest in front of Fort Emory (the one we built the first time that we went to the left, Jerry). The men are building commodious quarters, wood being plenty. Picket duty is very easy here, there being no enemy in sight. Some of the boys heard by letter of the fellows who died in the Bull pens of Georgia. It is terrible to think of, men of strong constitutions and muscular frames, in the prime of life, should die such a death. Starvation, for that is the death that I think they died of. Think of being penned up, dying inch by inch daily, and at last, rot to pieces. I can assure you I shall run a great risk of life before I shall be taken prisoner, for I consider that death is better than a southern Bull pen. It is very evident that Lawrence has a great deal to do with this regt. It is now called a Lawrence and Ipswich Regt. I think by seeing H's father about my case, or even getting some one in Lawrence to write, would be the best way to carry it through. But do it without my knowledge.

About my pictures, you did perfectly right, Susan Jane! Love to all

from Lev. Bradley, Jr.

P. S. Jerry, you might send me a V., which would be very acceptable.

[On December 7 he was in the engagement called "Weldon Raid," but he had stopped recording in his diary. Another soldier writes: "Supposing that the campaign was ended and that we were now to have winter quarters, the men went to work with a will, and in four days had put up comfortable log huts, all supplied with fireplace^; but on the Oth of December orders were rec'd to march at daylight. The men suffered severely on this raid, many of them coming back over frozen ground without shoes. The distance marched was ninety-six miles." Ed.]

CAMP 1ST MASS. H. ARTY., DEC. 31ST, 1864.

Dear Family:

I rec'd your last Sabbath letter, yesterday morn'g. It has been raining and snowing. I have but just returned from the Major's office, where I have been to report concerning the absence of men, preparatory to a muster for payment. This is the first time, for three years, that I have not made out the rolls; but my duties are such now that it would be impossible to do it. I have to drill recruits once a week, besides the regular forms and duties that it is necessary for us to go through, as soon as we come to a halt. Frank's letter I shall preserve with great care, or rather I wish you to. I shall enclose it with this, where you can let it remain. In years to come, if through the divine mercy of God, we are both permitted to live, it would doubtless be a pleasure to us both to look back to this his first letter. The wind has started up and it is snowing at a furious rate. Many of us are unprepared for it. My tent is quite comfortable, but I am forced to lay on the ground; wood is very scarce with us, having to back it almost a mile, and nothing but green pine at that. It will probably be drawn to us if we stop here any length of time. I am writing in great haste and in the cold, as you will plainly see by the writing. But come to look it over, as I have just done, it looks and reads a great deal worse than I expected; but I am forced to let it go, for this time, and in order to pass it by to my advantage, you will not consider it my weekly missive. Love to all from Lev.

[On January 1, 1865, he was promoted to orderly sergeant and had a furlough of ten days. Ed.]

CAMP IN THE FIELD, FEB. 12, 1865.

Dear Mother:

We were forced to come back from Washington by the Potomac river. There was but one Brigade in the fight [2nd Hatch's Run] last Sunday night, the 3rd of our division. They were charged three successive times by Divisions. And a fresh division each time. It is said that Genl. Lee commanded the movements in person. They intended to break our lines and by so doing, cut off the 5th Corps, which had gone out farther on the left. But they ran foul of fighting stock and were driven back with great loss. Our artillery was placed in such a position that it cut them up terribly,

Four men were found at the foot of a tree, all mangled up. The battery belonged to the " Old Bay State," viz. 10th Mass. I did not join the regt. till Thursday; I found them in a small pine thicket. The smoke was so dense as to be able to cut in slices. Our eyes were all blood shot. The old company was right glad to see me back. Do not take what I write as self esteem! It was proposed to give me three cheers; but the plan was abandoned much to my pleasure. All the time that I was gone there had been a perfect hubbub in the company. Sergt. D. not knowing human nature, swords had to be drawn one time. It was a great pleasure to me to be welcomed back the way I was. Every one had a good word to say to me. I pray God that I may always deal with men in such a manner that I may be looked up to as one possessing a whole soul, for it is a great pleasure to one to know that he is liked. And especially one placed as I am. We have moved every day since I got back. Yesterday our regt. with the 93rd N. Y. was on fatigue, slashing timber in front of works. It was splendid wood. I cannot imagine what farmers North would say to see the whole of an immense forest leveled in a day. We are lying now on a hill in an open field.

There is a good prospect of our going in to camp, but for how long no one knows. I have found all of my things well cared for, stove and all. I have slept well since I got back. Do not, I beg of you, feel any uneasiness on my account. What ever I need I will write for. I wish you would get some yarn or worsted and get one of the Dole's to knit me a sleeping cap; if they can't do it, get some one else. It would be a great comfort to me to have one, I have caught a cold already. I will do the honorable when I write to them. I enjoyed my furlough hugely; but bidding you all a long farewell marred the pleasure slightly. I beg of you again, do not worry for me; although life is uncertain, it is not necessary to borrow trouble. A great many of the regiments are without officers. By the last move, our lines have been lengthened three miles. We are ignorant of the genl. result of the move.

My regards to all enquiring friends, and love to all the Bradley family.

> Your dutiful son,
>
> Leverett Bradley, Jr.

P. S. Captain *[he always called his father that in these days]*, our men slightly wounded are falling off very fast. Co. B numbers only twenty-eight ready for duty. I wish you might get a place for me. I shall not expect one, because so many want them.

[He held the position of orderly sergeant, and was at many times commanding the company on account of the loss or absence of all commissioned officers. Ed.]

CAMP 1ST MASS. H. ART., MARCH 28, 1865.

Dear Jed:

I received your letter. I take this opportunity to answer, not knowing that I shall ever have another. We are under orders to move at 6 a.m. tomorrow; rations are being- drawn and other little matters attended to, but you know too well how this is all done. The Sith Corps is here with Sheridan's famous raiders and rumors have it that we are to join Sherman across the Country. I hope so for one; but it may only be a move for the south side of the R. R. The recommendations that you wished me to get for you have been obtained. I feel as though I must give you a little advice. Have you considered and made up your mind to give the rest of your years to your country? Either branches of the service are apt to lose their charm after a few years. It seems to me that you could choose some occupation or profession that you would be more capable of, and feel better satisfied with. I am willing, so far as it lays in my power, to do anything for you, even giving money for your advancement, of which you were robbed, by entering the service at so youthful an age. We can say that we passed three years in our country's service together. I will close now, to get a little sleep before tomorrow's movements. I beg of you now give this subject a long thought, for I think that your future depends upon it. You are moulding what is to be the man.

Give my love to all; please remember me to all enquiring friends.

Ever your brother,
L. Bradley, Jr.

[The battle of Vaughn Road was fought March 29, in which the regiment charged and took the first line of the enemy's works. On March 31 was the engagement at Burgess Mill. In this battle the First Massachusetts Heavy Artillery and the Fifth Michigan Infantry were ordered to charge a battery, protected by strong earthworks and heavy slashing, and it was in this charge that Leverett showed such bravery. It was later described by his captain, though he made nothing of it himself and I never heard him refer to it. Two days later, April 2, the whole line was ordered forward and the works were carried by assault. Captain Littlefield's account is of interest here. Ed.]

"I have the honor to state that the following describes the movements of portions of the 2nd Army Corps, on March 31, 1865, the 1st Mass. H. A. being in Mott's Division *[see Walker's Hist., 2nd Army Corps, page 663]*:

"General Humphreys had not limited his efforts for the support of Warren to the advance of Miles' division; but, immediately on learning that the enemy had assumed the offensive, he directed General Mott, if possible, to carry the entrenchments at Burgess' Mill and General Hayes to carry the Crow House redout. Neither of these assaults was successful, owing to the impenetrable abattis found along much of the line; but the attacks of Mott and Hayes were so close and persistent as to prevent the Confederates from reinforcing the troops in front of Warren and Miles, Genl. Wilcox, who commanded the line at Burgess' Mill and the Crow House, being compelled to refuse the Genl.'s request for an additional brigade.'

"Now at that time under consideration above, Sergeant Leverett Bradley, being in my immediate command, in moving forward to the abattis or slashing in solid mass, in front of the enemy's Avorks (some of my men failed at the onset to reach the outer edge of said slashing, but instead fell behind trees and commenced firing to the front, over the heads of the line advancing to the attack), the Sergeant, of his own motion, rallied these men into line, holding them there by his exhortation and example, when I addressed him in words of commendation for his brave act. Subsequently, just as we were mustered out, the Sergeant was commissioned First Lieut, by Governor Andrew of Mass., but our ranks had become so depleted it was consolidated with another command, so that this officer of gallant make-up could not be mustered to the grade he had exercised to all intents and purposes and been promoted to."
Roger S. Littlefield,

Jan. 28, 1895. Late captain 1st Mass. H. A.

CAMP IN THE FIELD, NEAR BURKSVILLE JUNCTION, VA.,

APRIL 17, 1865.

Dear Family:

We moved yesterday to this position, only a few rods from our former one, to wait orders. We rec'd the sad news of President Lincoln's being severely wounded in the head, yesterday morning, and of his death last night. The news cast a gloom upon all. Many were the oaths taken against the perpetrator of the deed. We rec'd no particulars, simply that it was by J. W. Booth in Ford's theatre, and that Sec'ty of State Mr. Seward and his son were attacked in their oviti house. We have had no newspapers of late date, since we left Petersburg, except the Richmond Whig, which goes on the same as before, with a great change in its tone. I will try now and give you a description of our operations, although I have no notes to copy from, I think it is impressed strongly enough upon my memory to transfer it to paper.

Sunday morning, Apr. 2nd, at about 7 o'clk our Regt. with the 5th Mich, filed out through the works into the woods on a double quick: all expected a repetition of the scene we passed through before, but what was our surprise, when we passed by the picket line, through the woods into an open field in full view of the Johnnies' works, and found them vacated. We immediately struck off in pursuit up the Boydton flank road, the sixth Corps in advance. The "Johns" made a stand about two miles from the City and the Artillery kept up the firing for the rest of the day. The next morning, we took the back road and struck out for the Danville road, which we reached the night of the 5th; fortified across it. Our Corps struck the Rebs the next day and gave them an awful run; they would make a stand on a hill, our skirmish line would run them out and then the Cavalry would give them a charge across the open country, till they found they had made another halt.

The road was strewn with cars, ammunition boxes, blankets, old broken down mules, horses and wagons, caissons, limbers, forges, and occasionally a gun. The men were all excitement over our late victories and nothing could stop them. Our Brigade captured seven flags. Our regt. was unlucky and got none. We followed them up this way till the surrender. I have never seen such a sight and never expect to, as I did when Genl. Meade rode in from the front and a staff officer announced that Lee had surrendered [the surrender of General Lee at Appomattox Court House]. The men hurrahed as if their throats would split. Soon after Meade came riding through the lines. All the flags were given to the breeze and the men crowded around them and cheered lustily, rushing after Genl. Meade all the time. Men threw up their caps, haversacks, and canteens and some even took off their shoes and threw them up, running a great risk of ever getting them again. Every one had a smile on his face, although they had been without rations for a day and a half.

                                              Regards and love to all. Lev.

Camp 1st Mass. H. Arty., near Burksville Junction, Va.,
Apr. 20, 1865.

Dear Jed:

I have been at work all the afternoon fixing up our tent. I have seen considerable within the last few weeks; when we first struck the "John Henrys "and had followed them a few miles, we began to pick up the relics by the bushels, a great many of which had to be thrown away, as the marches were so severe that the men had rather keep their tack; but we had but little of that. I have got a Confederate States Army Regulations. We are just getting the news of the surrender of Johnson to Sherman. The boys say be ready to meet them at the depot with your drums about the 4th July. They begin to feel more homesick; they feel they have done their duty and now want to go home. Some 60 cannon were dug up near the station today, which the Rebs buried, and placed head boards at the head of the graves; some were Sergts, corpls. &c., quite a joke! Our Co. (just previous to our first move from camp) was changed from the third to the Second Batt.

Our U. S. colors got torn all to pieces in our late scrap, and shell broke the staff in three pieces and tore the flag from the staff. We pitch our tent this time as we used to last summer, high, and then build a bunk of poles. We have got a gay one. We have three wool blankets and are hunky! None of us expect any more fighting. I got a chronicle of our new president's plans and views, the most noticeable being, "treason must be punished." I feel that the South were interested in the late assassination. It will avail them nothing; but will rather injure them. T think they can well say that this is a curious army; a foreign one would have massacred the inhabitants on receiving the news that we rec'd, but with us it was all quiet. Tell mother my catarrh is all right. Give my regards to all the boys and gals.

love to all. Lev.

CAMP 1ST MASS. H. A., NEAR BURKSVILLE JUNCTION, VA.,

APRIL 26, 1865.

Dear Family:

Yours of the 19th has been rec'd. Yesterday was a holiday with us, opening with a salute of thirteen guns, and a gun every half hour during the day, with a National salute of thirty six guns at sunset. We were paraded at 10 A.M. and the orders of the Sect'y of war and Lieut Genl. Grant were read to us. All the men are dissatisfied, stopping here in camp. The army of the Potomac is without an enemy in front, and we lay here waiting orders. I think that the views of President Johnson are very different from what the late old Abe's were, in regard to the settlement of this great rebellion for which so many lives have been sacrificed. I favor the former's views, i. e., "Treason is a crime and must be punished." I hardly think the war worn veterans would be satisfied luiless it was done. Genl. Lee must be made an example of immediately and all other Generals in our hands, particularly those who have ever meddled with politics, should suffer their fate. I can't bring my thoughts to believe that we are soon to go home; but our minds are at ease about fighting. We are expecting good news from Genl. Sherman, but yesterday's paper had particulars of his negotiation, which has lowered him in my estimation: but "Old Useless" himself has gone down to North Carolina to run the machine. The sun is hot enough to cook coffee in the open air. It is nearly a year since I went home on my veteran furlough, and how many scenes of strife and bloodshed I have since passed through. I had a small idea of the army then; but now I think

I can well say that I have been through the mill. F. P., who left us last fall when there was fighting, has returned with Capt's bars. I assure you he was not welcome amongst those who had done their duty at the front to the present time. I was witness to a big nigger fight last night. They were passed round through the crowd in a hurry. If you have any old magazines about the house, please send them to me, as reading matter is scarce.

Respectfully yours,
L. Bradley, Jr., 1st Sergt. Co. B.

CAMP 1ST H. ARTY., NEAR ARLINGTON MILLS, VA.,
MAY 24, 1865.

Dear Family:

I have hardly kept my promise about writing; but I hope you will excuse me, for we have slept most of the time since we got into camp. We lay on a ridge right near the old mill, a mile from the road in a splendid oak grove. It has rained for three days and we hope that it will clear before tomorrow; for on Tuesday we are to be reviewed in Washington. We all dread the march, for it will be a long one and if it should be hot, many will faint. We have begun making out the muster rolls for the men whose term of service expires before Oct. 1st. If you should hear the stories that we have' in camp you would laugh out right. One (lay, they are favorable for the recruits, and the next, for the veterans. Now Mother I hope you will feel easy about me, at least for the present till we hear what they intend to do with the veterans. We draw soft bread every day now and vegetables are more plentiful than at the front. George Frye [the cousin who was taken prisoner] has got back to the regt. now, looking finely. The country along the road has changed a great deal and it is lined with sutlers' shanties. Some of the 4th " Heavies ' ' have been up here; they look as if they had been playing soldiers for a while.

A year ago I was enjoying myself at home among friends and relatives. It does seem as if I never felt happier till 1 heard that the regiment had lost such numbers. I was shown the very tree where George Bricket and others sat under a few hours before that awful fight [the Wilderness]. I should have gone to the ground itself; but we were moving on another road, until it made a junction with the main road, three miles from the battle field. The thunder is beginning again; we were caught in that terrible one, just after leaving Falmouth. The trial of the assassins is developing a great many important facts which the government intend to take advantage of.

I wish they would bring Jeb to Washington in the same clothes that they caught him in.

With much love to all, I remain as ever,
Leverett Bradley, Jr.

Camp 1st Mass. H. A., May 29.

Dear Family:

Your last was rec'd. The great review^ has passed, it was a beautiful day. The Regt. was composed of six companies. I was the left guide of the color Co.; many were the remarks about our tattered banners. The ladies kept their handkerchiefs going all the time. I should have thought they would have got tired by night. The streets were crowded full to over flowing. The absorbing topic is when are we to be discharged H Jerry, I hear stories of your flirtations out here. George, now you are 21, you should make your appearance with a tall hat, cigar in your mouth, a fighting dog under your carriage; try and keep up to the times; wait till I get home and then there will be no chance for you, better get married now. News is so scarce with us that it is hard to make up a letter. The boys sleep most of the 24 hours.

As ever, Lev.

Camp 1st H. A., June 4, 1865.

Dear Family:

We had inspection this morning. I had command of the Co. We have got a new State Color, a perfect beauty! We are waiting for a new national one from the government. The old ones, that stood the brunt of so many battles, are now almost in shreds and have been packed up ready to transmit to Adjt. Genl. of the state soon; if we are not soon to go home, in which case we shall carry them. The review of the corps came off. It was not as severe as we expected. Genl. Hancock looked admirably and rec'd cheers.

The 6th Corps' Artillery is coming in now, on a road to the left of us; the horses look played out, leaning against each other for support. Every day Ave hear cheers in some camp regiment whose time is out in Oct. and now about to start for home. Candle light parades are beginning to be a great feature of military and camp illuminations. The scenes are beautiful to look at, but not so agreeable to participate in, grease not being an ornament to clothes. Clothing has just come, so I shall have to make larger letters or write faster to finish up. If it is a scrawl, my thoughts are all there, which is all that is required.

With love to all, Lev. B., Jr.

I presume that it is proper that you, Lizzie, should give away my photographs.

FORT ETHAN ALLEN, VA., JUNE 18, 1865.

Dear Family:

Your last rec'd. It does seem as if the flies would eat me up!!! and as for bed bugs, we caught them by the peck this afternoon. We relieved the 6th Penn H. A. I went to work, white washed my room and scalt the bunk; but from the rest I got last night should say that there are bed bugs yet.

Lt. Col. Shatswell is Commanding the Brig, but our Regt. is at present the only one in it; he is entitled the same however to a staff and orderlies. I know you would not expect me to write if you saw how the flies trouble me, so will close for now, or go into spasms. L. Bradley, Jr.

Fort Ethan Allen, Va., June 25, 1865.

Dear Friends:

Four years ago yesterday, this Co. left the pleasant village of Methuen, for Fort Warren; there to be drilled and disciplined for war. Some went out of pure patriotism and others out of curiosity, they knew little of war; but they all had drawn a picture of it in their minds and I think their conclusions fell far short of the mark. For my own part, I feel glad that we were ordered from the forts about Washington. What I have seen and learned, money cannot buy. But to think that we have lost so many of our brave comrades by this cruel rebellion (many of them friends of mine) is enough to make all cry " Peace" and no more "War." I thank God I was allowed to pass through so many bloody scenes. Life seemed of but little importance to me; but I never yet gave up and who knows but that was the reason I was allowed to live f I shall send you a copy of Genl. Pierce's Order. We were a favorite regt. of his. The 5th Michigan and 1st Massachusetts H. A. ha\e fought side by side in many a battle and I have often heard the Genl. say "two better Regts. could not be found in the service."

We were always taken when an object of importance was to be obtained, and they always showed themselves true soldiers. The work of mustering out veteran troops has begun; we think we should have gone if we had remained in the Corps. The weather has been terribly hot the past week, but the flies are not so bad since the food has been moved into the mess house. Bed bugs are as bad as ever, I cannot sleep in my bunk, but take a couple of chairs and like it much better. I earnestly hope, Jerry, that you will succeed in getting into the naval school, if you have made up your mind. You must not let father work so hard; just take command and have discipline in the house hold. Give my love to all. Hoping to help you gather the harvest this fall, I remain, T.. Bradley, Jr.

[Copy of General Pierce's Order.]
EXTRACT FROM
SPECIAL ORDERS, NO. 166.
HEADQUARTERS 2ND BRIGADE, 3RD DIVISION,
2D ARMY CORPS, JUNE 15, 1865.

4. The 1st Mass. H. A. having been ordered to report to Genl. Hancock, the Genl. commanding, on parting with them, desires to express his heartfelt thanks for their general good conduct while under his command. Although entering the field in the summer of 1864, at the height of the most severe campaign the army ever had, they showed by their daring bravery and gallant charges, that they had been drilled and disciplined for a purpose. Their now disseminated ranks attest the valor and patriotic spirit with which they were inspired. He has every reason to feel proud of their conduct both in camp and on the battle-field and shall ever remember with pleasure their connection and association with the Brigade, with which their military history has now become a part.

By command of
Brig. Genl. Pierce.
(Signed) C. W. Forrester,
Capt. and A. A. A. G.
FORT ETHAN ALLEN, VA., JUNE 19, 1865.

LEVERETT BRADLEY, 1ST SERGT.

FORT C. F. SMITH, VA.. JULY 2, 1865.

Dear Friends:

The men like it here, for the duty is much easier. We relieved some of the N. Y. Arty. Three companies are in a barrack, draw rations and mess together. I never felt it so warm.

Nearly every afternoon I sit and let the perspiration drop from my chin; a very agreeable occupation. Some of the regts. in our old corps had a row yesterday, refusing to do duty. I don't know how they came out in the matter. I should like to be with you the coming fourth. I know nothing for us to do but sit still and think of what a good time you are having. We have a fine view of Washington, Georgetown, Chain bridge and the upper Potomac. One man is allowed to visit Washington daily. The boys have got up a new game of cards, played like muggins; but the one that is beaten has to allow the rest to give him three raps each, across the nose; it leaves a very peculiar tingling sensation after the operation and makes any amount of sport. D. has been reduced to the ranks for abusive language. Jerry will tell you about the man the men have been under. We were mustered for pay by Maj. H 1. The men are improving in looks greatly. Putting on our fortification airs now, Sarvy!

Much love to all,
L. Bradley, Jr.

Monday Morning. Had for breakfast one cup of coffee and one slice of bread. I assure you, we fat on the living !

[On July 11 he was 19 years old. Ed.]

FORT MORTON, VA., JULY 16.

Dear Friends:

I am beginning this letter under adverse circumstances, for we have just rec'd an order to be ready to move immediately back to Fort Smith, where all the Cos. of the regt. are to concentrate. It is beautifully situated here. We have just got everything going smoothly, our Co. being here alone, so still, and we feel vexed at having to go back. I visited Washington last night; went to the theatre, and liked it.

There is a guitar in my window which the wind is playing splendidly. My mind is nowhere today. Regts. pass here every morning on their way home. We are all in hopes our turn will come soon.

This letter contains all the news I can collect; but at that in a consolidated form. Love to all from L. Bradley, Jr.

[There now comes a disappointment which he bore uncomplainingly and accepted as the inevitable. It was not until 1895, when urged by men in Philadelphia and by his wife, that he made a slight effort, by going to Washington, to see if the matter could be rectified. He was convinced that it was of too slight importance to interest the Senate, and would probably be defeated promptly, as the tendency was to cut down claims which might establish a precedent at that late date. The following gives the statement of his former colonel. Ed.]

To whom it may concern:

I, Nathanial Shatswell, do hereby certify that I served in the 1st Mass. H. A. during the war of the Rebellion, and that during the last fifteen months of the war I was its commander. I knew Leverett Bradley, Jr., who served in Co. B of the Regiment for the four years or more of the war, and while I commanded the Regiment I knew him well. He entered the army at the tender age of fifteen, serving- faithfully and honorably until his discharge. He filled the positions of the Company Quartermaster-Sergeant and 1st Sergeant to the satisfaction of his superiors and to the advantage of the country. He received a commission as 1st Lieut, in the Regiment from the Governor of Mass., dated July 31, 180.5, and his name appears in the records of the state credited with that rank.

I learn that the War Department at Washington declines to muster him upon this commission (though he seeks the muster only that he may be eligible to membership in the Loyal Legion), because there was no vacancy of his grade in the Regiment at the time. The absence of vacancy is, of course, a matter of record and need not be gainsaid. But the causes which led to this condition of things in a regiment which lost heavily, and at times had merely a handful of officers, may be of some interest. Had the Regiment been mustered out of service in the condition that it was a month after the surrender of Lee there would have been vacancies, and many in the grade of 1st Lieut., and Lieut. Bradley would have found no difficulty in obtaining an order for muster from the War Department. But after that date, a month or more after the close of the fighting. Col. Wm. F. Abert. commanding the 3rd Mass. H. A., a regiment which never smelled smoke of battle, conceived the idea of having the 12 companies of the 1st Regt. consolidated into 4 companies and thus the Regiment into a battalion, and of having tins battalion attached to his command. An order to this effect was issued from the War Department. It caused me great bitterness of heart to execute the command, but I obeyed my instructions. The 12 companies of my command were consolidated into 4 companies. This action easily and necessarily filled all vacancies in the various grades among the commissioned officers. At this point I was so deeply affected by the discredit which would be done to a regt. which had seen service through the war by assigning it as a battalion to a command which had made for itself no name, I determined to do all in my power to save it from destruction and to perpetuate its identity. I therefore consulted the Hon. Henry Wilson, senator from Massachusetts, and laid the whole matter before him, pleading that the Regt. might be honorably discharged under the name which it had so honorably borne; soon after an order came down from the War Department countermanding the order for consolidation with the 3rd Mass., and ordering the Regt. to Ije honorably discharged. The Regt. Was discharged and disbanded on Aug. 16, 1865.

Now, it can easily be seen that the order for the consolidation of 12 companies into 4 companies was an unnecessary one, and considering the History of the Regiment, an unfair and unjust one. Had there been no such consolidation there would have been many vacancies in the grade of 1st Lieut., enabling the said Leverett Bradley, Jr., to be mustered.

Thirty years have passed since the Regiment was discharged, and I may be said to be somewhat sobered by age. But I deliberately place on record my profound and settled conviction that a grievous and cruel and useless order was issued when I was commanded to consolidate my 12 companies into 4 companies. But whether this is true or not, I know that the consolidation deprived Lieut. Bradley of the right and privilege of muster into the U. S. service under the commission given by the Governor of Mass., a commission which the said Lieut. Bradley won by honorable and efficient service. He was a true and good soldier, faithful, obedient, intelligent and brave, and deserves such consideration at the hands of those who can grant it as shall place his name among the commissioned officers of the 1st

Mass. H. A. Nathanial Shatswell.

September, 1895.

1st Sergt's Office.

Co. B 1st Mass. H. A., Fort Bunker Hill, D. C,

Aug. 6, 1865.

Dear Friends:

Your last found me in tolerable good health. I am now fairly at work in my new duties. I assure you it is a different thing to have two strange companies, old soldiers at that, with the old Company to handle, from what it was before. I contend that the 1st Sergt's position at present in the four companies is the hardest position in the Regt.; but so far I am doing finely.

Four years ago yesterday, I left the old parental roof for the first time, for a commencement in life. At other times people might say I chose a very dangerous life; but a desire to be a soldier had got possession of me and I actually believe if I had not been allowed to come at that time I should have come on my own responsibility soon after. How fortunate I have been during these last four years. I have suffered but little from sickness. The hardships have been severe, to be sure, for the last year; but life has been spared. I look back at times and think how I suffered a year ago from long marches, hunger, thirst, and fatigue, and shudder at the thought of a repetition of the scenes.

A great many of the boys have acted foolishly since pay day by deserting; you have probably seen some of them. A man must be crazy that would act so. I feel as if I would like an honorable discharge after serving faithfully almost four years. I should like to know well what kind of business it was you would like me to go into, if I got a discharge. Money making of course . I should advise Jerry to give way and let George visit Washington, and shall urge his coming; he has never travelled and if he could possibly be spared I think he ought to take a short trip this way. Perhaps he has struck higher and prefers to visit Saratoga or Niagara Falls! The 3rd Regt. has not been consolidated yet; they are waiting the arrival of a company from Richmond. We all hope the consolidation will never come off. Hard feelings are beginning to exist between the two Regts. already. We are expecting daily to lose our colors, now in Washington, having the names of the battles we were in printed on it, as the guard has been discontinued. Some of their companies will probably have the honor of carrying the Colors. Perhaps it isn't rough, but we can't see it in that light! We are in hopes that Col. A. will be sent back to the Regular Army and N. promoted; then we would have our slow at every thing.

Aug. 7.

I wish it were so I could get home soon and then all take a short trip to the beach. We never went to but few places as a whole family. I board out now; about eight of us draw our rations and have a woman to cook for us, and with a few bought articles we live tolerably well. Report says we are going soon to some other station. I can see no necessity of staying here, as there is no armament.

Love to all. Lev. Bradley, Jr.

FORT BUNKER HILL, D. C, AUG. 11, 1865.

Dear Family:

It is with the greatest pleasure that I take my pen to inform you of our immediate muster out of service. Although you will probably get the news from the papers long before this reaches you. Although the duties will not devolve upon me to make out the rolls, I feel it my duty to all that I should render my whole assistance, having full as good knowledge of Company affairs as any person. I flatter myself that Old Co. B will not be in the rear in completing the rolls, which are expected back this evening. And then! Won't pen, ink and paper have to take up? I feel much that Col. Shatswell selected me as one to remain, although at the time I felt much mortified. I told him so yesterday. He is highly pleased to find matters turning out as they are. We shall carry two sets of colors, the old tattered ones and the new ones with sixteen battles inscribed upon its silken folds! I shall box up all my clothing, books &c.. and try to get it along as company baggage; but if not successful shall forward by ex. Can't some of you meet us at Boston, when we first arrive, and have a woolen blanket with you for me to take to Readville in case I am unable to get my box along; for I expect it will be cooler than here. Imagine my feelings at the present moment, waiting patiently for the rolls to come so as to begin to write myself " out of service"! I feel sorry for those that have deserted; it must be a severe blow to know we are coming home soon. I shall do all I can in trading, as an excellent opportunity offers itself. If a better chance offered to get horses home and I was a little better judge of horse flesh myself, I should, I think, try to trade a little.

With love to all, I remain the same Lev.

[Like many another, he was glad to be a private citizen again; but it was characteristic of him that he turned at once to other work, and took no thought of that which he had done. Referring to some gathering of the Grand Army, he writes to his mother in 1890: "I'm a poor old soldier, but cannot enthuse

over such a gathering nor lend my presence to its success, except as a spectator. I have no objection to old soldiers getting together, if they wish to do so; but I do quietly object to their claiming the cessation of the trade and the sympathy of the public. The War is a memory; a precious one to some of us. There is nothing to be gained by our strutting as old soldiers before the youth of the land. They must read of the war to understand it. I 'm afraid I 'm a mugwump and that old soldiers will call me one. No good nor high end is in view to elevate the thoughts and actions of the encampment. Personal glory and advantages to be won are too conspicuous in the whole undertaking to please me." Ed.]

www.ingramcontent.com/pod-product-compliance
Lightning Source LLC
Chambersburg PA
CBHW031410040426
42444CB00005B/494